CW00503060

TUNING LUCAS IGNITION SYSTEMS

speedsport motobooks

First impression November 1972

ISBN 0 85113 06 3 1

Published by
Speedsport Motobooks
(Interauto Book Company Limited)
Bercourt House, York Road, Brentford,
Middlesex, TW8 OQP, England

Printed in Great Britain by
HGA Printing Company Ltd.,
Brentford, Middlesex

TUNING LUCAS IGNITION SYSTEMS

CONTENTS

Chapter 1

Ignition Coil - How it works

Petrol vapour mixed with air in a conventional piston engine forms a combustible gas which normally requires some form of spark to ignite it. The heat generated in compressing the mixture during the four-stroke cycle is insufficient to cause spontaneous combustion, and only the diesel engine (which has a much higher compression ratio) manages to rely on spontaneous ignition. In the petrol engine, a sparking plug is provided for each cylinder and an electro-mechanical system is arranged to cause ignition at a very carefully timed moment, the efficient and smooth running of the engine being entirely dependent upon exactly when the spark occurs.

Although some forms of basic engine, as used in motorcycles and lawn-mowers, have self-energising ignition devices called magnetos, the modern car utilises its main battery as the source of energy for the spark. In all but a very few examples this is a 12 volt unit. For there to be a discharge (and hence a spark) across the gap between the two electrodes of the sparking plug, a potential difference of about 10,000 volts is required, so a compact and efficient transformer called the coil is inserted in the circuit. It steps up the low-tension voltage from the battery by means of electrical induction pulses, these being caused by a make-and-break device in the primary low-tension circuit known as the contact breaker. It is located in the distributor.

The distributor has two other very important functions. It controls the timing of the spark to each cylinder, varying this with engine speed and load to give the smoothest and most efficient running, and at the same time it distributes the high voltage which causes the spark to the correct cylinder for each pulse in the cycle. In the ignition system the distributor is the most complicated unit and, because it contains moving parts, it is the only unit which requires routine maintenence. It is the commonest source of trouble in the ignition system for the same reason.

The elements contained in the ignition system are therefore the 12-volt battery which supplies the energy at one end and the sparking plugs which provide ignition in the cylinders at the other. In between there is the coil to step up the low-tension voltage of the battery to high-tension sufficient to jump the sparking plug gap and the distributor, which provides carefully-timed low-tension pulses to the coil and directs the high-tension surge to the correct cylinder at the best moment in the cycle. All modern cars for several years now have been designed with the negative terminal of the battery connected to "earth", this term being applied to the common steel structure of the car including the engine block which forms a return path for any electrical component connected to the positive or power side of the battery.

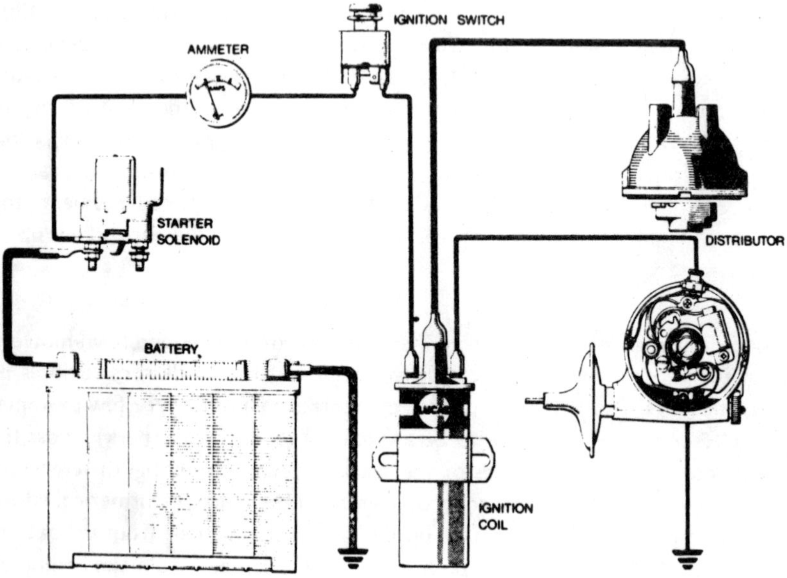

Fig. 1.1 - Typical ignition system showing the positions of the main components in the circuits.

Low-tension 12-volt supply is through normal small-gauge non-tinned stranded copper wire insulated with PVC and the high-tension supply is through either similar copper wire with thick insulation or graphite-impregnated rayon braid in the same kind of sleeving. Low tension connections are by means of spade-type Lucar clips, while high-tension connections are by means of cylindrical plugs crimped to the sleeving after the wire has been turned back over the outside or a staple inserted up the centre.

When current is flowing through the primary winding of the coil, a strong magnetic field exists around it. Interrupting the flow with the contact breaker in the distributor causes the magnetic field to collapse and when this happens a high voltage is induced in the secondary winding of the coil, which is then fed to the distributor and each sparking plug in turn. The efficiency of the system depends on how rapidly the magnetic field collapses and to achieve the desired characteristics a capacitor or condenser is connected in parallel with the contact breaker points.

To eliminate the problems of contact breaker points pitting, a new type of circuit using transistors as high-speed solid-state switches is available. It is known as the Lucas T.A.C. (transistor assisted contacts) system and with it there is negligible arcing at the contacts. These therefore require much less attention at routine intervals, and their life is extended considerably. This system is not fitted as initial equipment yet, but is available as an accessory for converting existing systems.

Because the timing of the spark in each cycle of the engine is critical, any maladjustment of the distributor or fault in the electrical part of the system will cause a loss in the performance of the vehicle both in terms of power developed and fuel consumption. Before making any adjustments to carburetters or carrying out any modifications to the head or induction system it is vital that the ignition system is given a thorough check-up and passed out with a clean bill of health. In the following chapters I shall examine each component part of the ignition system in detail and explain how to check that it is functioning correctly. Then I shall take a look at the special ignition requirements of high-performance engines and how these can be provided when making modifications to more ordinary units. Finally I shall explain how to set up an ignition system correctly with ordinary inexpensive equipment and then how to locate and cure ignition troubles.

Chapter 2

The Coil Itself - Function and Troubleshooting

As already mentioned, the coil is a kind of very compact transformer which boosts the 12-volt low-tension voltage of the battery to over 10,000 volts for the high-tension discharge that causes the plug to spark. It has no mechanical moving parts, two sets of windings and a laminated iron core being sealed in an aluminium can with an insulated top.

For a voltage to be induced in a coil, lines of magnetic force must pass across the wire, this principle being used to generate current in a dymano, the armature moving past magnetic poles in the casing. In an a.c. transformer, the alternating current reverses the polarity of the iron core each time it changes direction in the primary coil, inducing a voltage in the secondary. The step-up or step-down of the voltage depends upon the relative number of turns in each winding respectively. In circuit with a.c. primary winding of the coil in a car is a make-and-break device (the contacts in the distributor) which causes the magnetic field around the iron core to collapse and reform. As the lines of magnetic force move across the secondary winding, a voltage is induced in it.

The heart of the coil is a laminated iron core upon which are wound about 20,000 turns of fine (44swg) enamel-covered wire, each layer being insulated from the next by a thin paper strip. Around the outside, further insulated by varnished paper, are about 300 turns of much thicker (25swg) enamel-covered wire in three layers. A slotted iron sheath goes round the outer windings and the whole assembly is then inserted into an aluminium can with a porcelain base support. Originally the windings were wax impregnated and the can filled with pitch to "pot" the components and prevent them being affected by vibration. Air bubbles often caused failures, so these days the coil is filled with insulating oil which helps in the dissipation of heat.

Called the primary winding, the outer coils of wire are connected to two low-tension terminals on top of the insulated cap. These are marked with a "+" and a "-", or with the initials SW (for ignition switch) and CB (for contact breaker). When the contact breaker in the distributor is closed, the circuit from the battery through the coil to the earth of the engine is complete. and a magnetic field is formed around the iron core of the coil. When the contact breaker opens, the circuit is no longer complete and the current ceases to flow. With no current in

Fig. 2.1 - Ignition coil with blade connectors for the low-tension primary circuit and a central chimney for the high-tension secondary output.

the primary circuit, the magnetic field collapses and as it does so the wires of the secondary coil are cut by lines of magnetic force, thus inducing a potential difference in the secondary winding, which is connected through the distributor to each plug in turn. This surge causes a high voltage spark to jump the gap between the electrodes of the sparking plug, igniting the mixture in the process.

Fig. 2.2 - Cutaway section of the coil showing the construction and insulation of the windings.

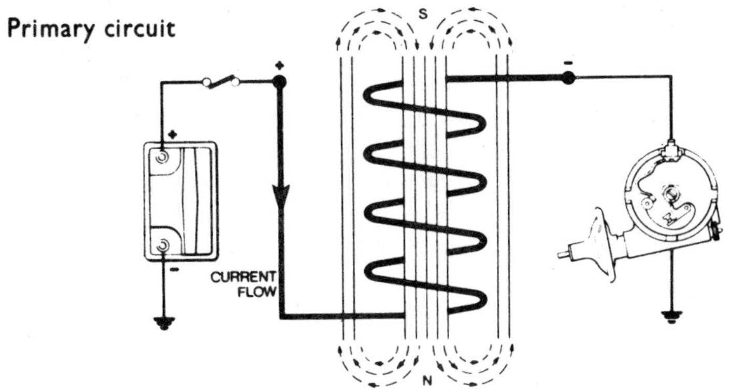

Fig. 2.3 - Primary low-tension circuit with current flowing and a magnetic field generated in the core of the coil.

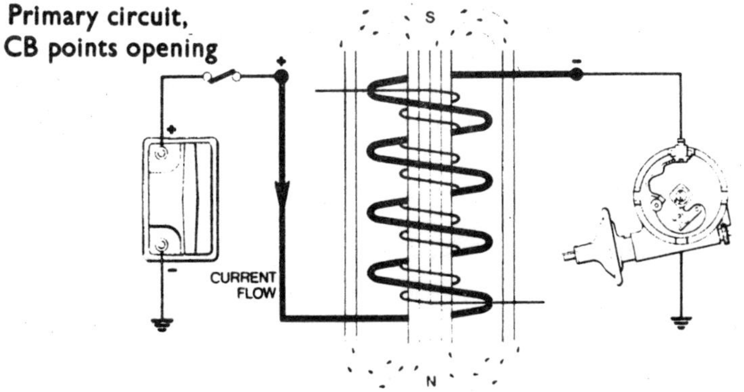

Fig. 2.4 - When the contact breaker points open the magnetic field collapses, inducing a back emf in both the primary and secondary circuits.

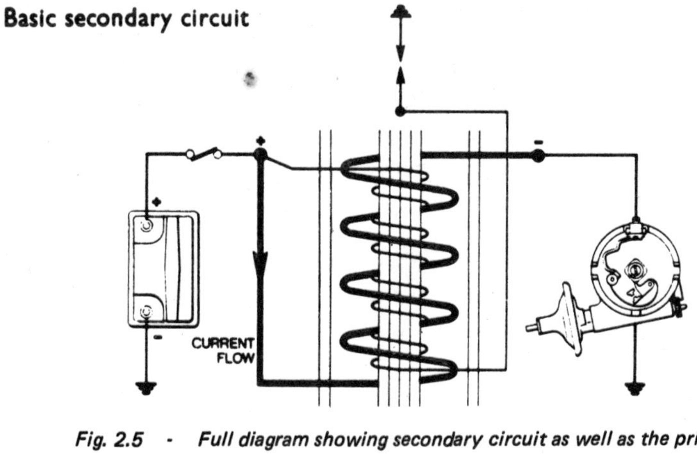

Fig. 2.5 - Full diagram showing secondary circuit as well as the primary.

The rate at which this magnetic field collapses controls the voltage induced in the secondary circuit to a very large extent and to increase this a capacitor is connected in parallel across the contact breaker points. When the contacts open, instead of the primary current attempting to continue across them, it switches to the alternative path through the capacitor and the self-induced primary current (caused by the collapse of the coil's magnetic field) charges the capacitor instead of causing arcing across the points. Thus although the ignition system might work without a capacitor, the induced voltage would be drastically reduced and there would be excessive arcing at the contact breaker points. In time, this arcing would cause the effective contact gap to close up by transfering tiny particles of metal from one face to the other and forming a resistive oxide layer.

Primary Circuit

The low-tension primary circuit starts at the battery and connects via the starter switch with the control box. Unusually this first stage of the car's wiring loom is shared with most of the other electrical accessories. From the control box the circuit runs through the ignition switch to the positive (on a car with negative earth) low-tension terminal on top of the coil. From the negative terminal a low-tension wire runs to the side of the distributor body and thence inside to the contact breaker, which is earthed to the engine block. For checking the primary circuit a voltmeter is needed, with wander leads ending in crocodile clips.

Starting at the battery side of the coil (marked SW or + on cars with a negative earth), connect the voltmeter between this point and a good earth, such as a stud on the block or the earthing strap if it is the exposed braided type. The contacts can be open or closed, but it is preferable to have them closed so that current flows in the primary circuit. If a reading equal to the battery voltage is obtained with the ignition switched on, all is well in this part of the primary circuit. If no reading is obtained there is a break in the wiring somewhere between the control box and the coil. For this test of continuity in the low resistance part of the circuit, a 12-volt bulb can be used for testing if a voltmeter is not available.

If all is well in the supply of current to the coil, the next thing to check is the primary winding. The contacts in the distributor must be open for this test, so turn the engine slightly if they were closed for the previous check. The voltmeter should now be connected between the CB or "-" terminal and earth.

With the ignition switched on there should be a reading equal to battery voltage.

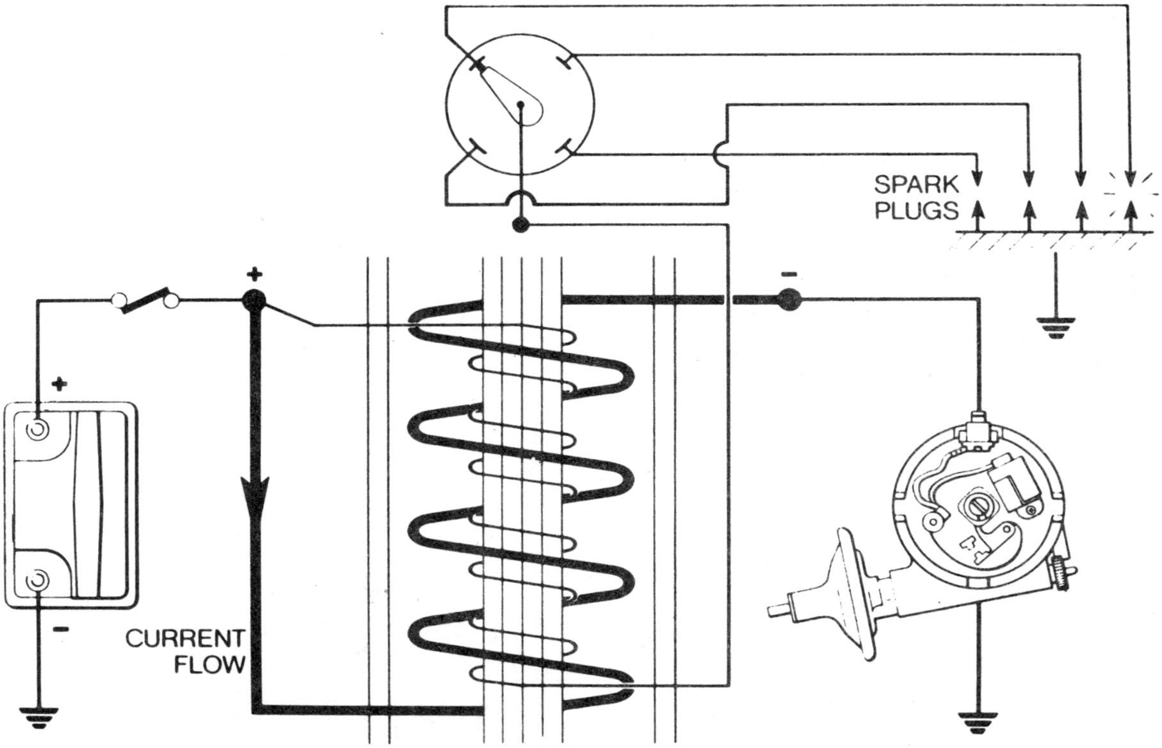

Fig. 2.6 - Circuit diagram of the ignition system with the two functions of the distributor separated into the primary and secondary circuits.

If the voltmeter reads zero, there is either a break in the primary winding of the coil or a short-circuit to earth in the distributor.

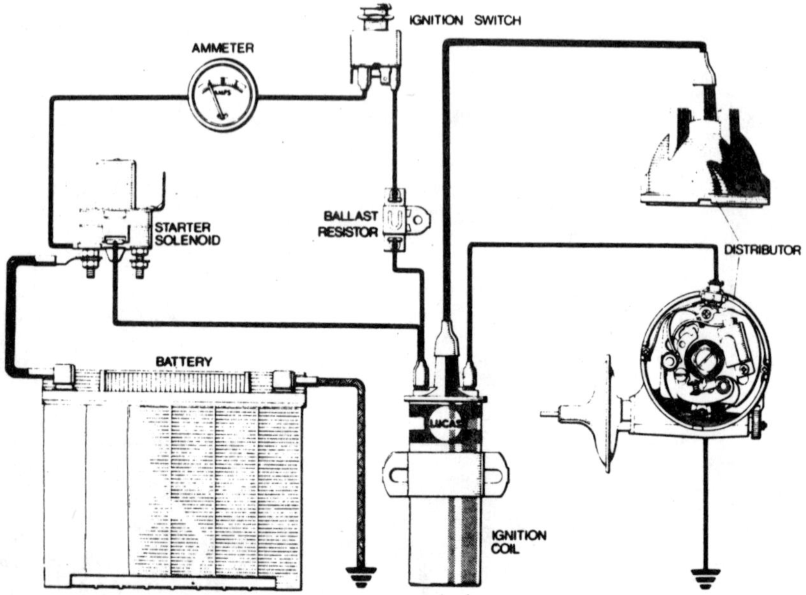

Fig. 2.7 - Typical ballasted ignition system as used on most modern cars as an aid to easy starting.

To determine which fault is present, remove the low tension lead from the coil at the CB or "-" terminal, but leave the voltmeter connected to the coil. If the voltmeter still reads zero, the primary winding is broken. If battery voltage registers as soon as the lead is removed, there is a short to earth in the distributor. The latter will be dealt with in Chapter 3.

Secondary Circuit

If all the checks on the primary circuit show no fault, the secondary circuit should next be tested to see whether sufficient voltage is being induced to provide a spark across the plug electrodes. A form of adjustable gap is needed for this test, together with a length of high-tension lead which can be fitted into the central chimney of the coil. With the ignition switched on and the distributor contacts closed, a spark of ¼in. should be obtained between the H.T. lead and earth each time the contacts are flicked open. If there is no spark and the primary circuit has been checked and found O.K., the secondary winding may be broken or be open-circuit.

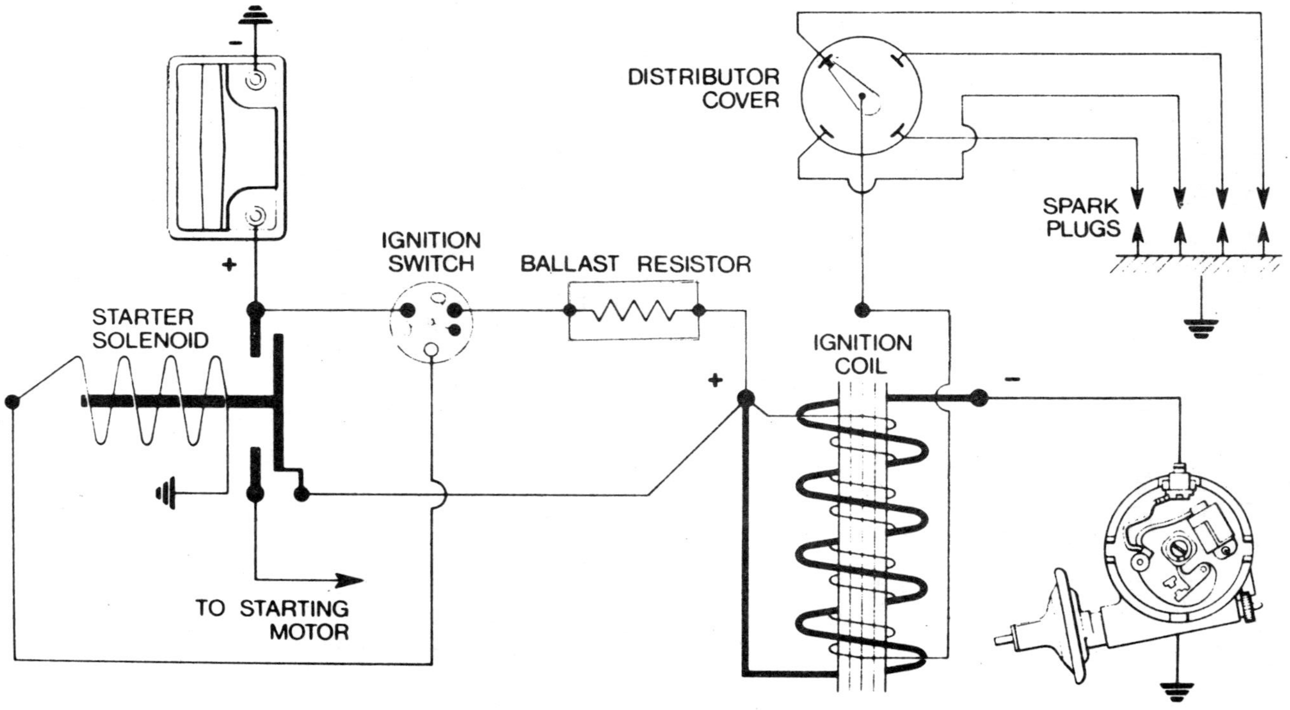

Fig. 2.8 - Ballasted ignition circuit. When the starter switch is operated the ballast resistor is shorted out, thus boosting the primary voltage to the coil.

Chapter 3

Distributors - Contact Breaker, Centrifugal and Vacuum Advance, Condenser and Insulation

As mentioned earlier, the distributor has three separate functions to perform. It contains and operates the make-and-break device for the primary circuit; it distributes the high-tension voltage to whichever plug is required to spark; and it controls the timing of the spark according to engine speed and load.

Mechanically the distributor comprises a fixed housing inside which is a shaft driven by the engine at half crankshaft speed, usually by skew gears from the camshaft. For the make-and-break device a pair of contacts are arranged so that a four-lobe cam (for a typical four-cylinder four-stroke engine) on the distributor shaft opens them against spring pressure provided by a single curved blade. The shape of the cam ramps is designed to open the contacts quickly and cleanly, after they have been closed long enough for the magnetic field to build up sufficiently in the coil. The part of each revolution during which the contacts are closed is known as the dwell angle and it is set by adjusting the gap between the points when they are open their full distance (i.e. the heel of the cam follower is on the peak of the cam lobe). A slotted hole in the fixed contact attachment is provided so that the gap can be adjusted. For the ignition system to work correctly the faces of the contacts must be clean, dry and aligned correctly and the gap set to the prescribed distance within specified limits. By far the commonest cause of non-starting, misfiring or poor performance and fuel consumption is neglect of the contact breaker points. Because the rest of the ignition system runs without maintenance, the distributor is often ignored.

One of the most vital parts in the distributor assembly is therefore the contact breaker. It is mounted on a base plate which itself is free to move in relation to the distributor body, this movement however being carefully controlled. A short link connects the base plate with a sealed diaphragm, the opposite side being subjected to induction vacuum by a small-bore pipe usually tapped into the carburetter body. Since engine vacuum is proportional to load, this mechanism provides a measure of adjustment to the ignition timing according to how hard the engine is working.

Independently of the base plate, the cam can also rotate by a small amount on the distributor shaft, this motion being controlled by a centrifugal spring mechanism which advances the timing in proportion to engine speed. Such is the nature of the combustion in the cylinder (see Appendix I) that the speed at which the flame spreads from the spark remains the same as the engine speeds up, thus requiring progressively more advance to reduce the emission of unburnt fuel.

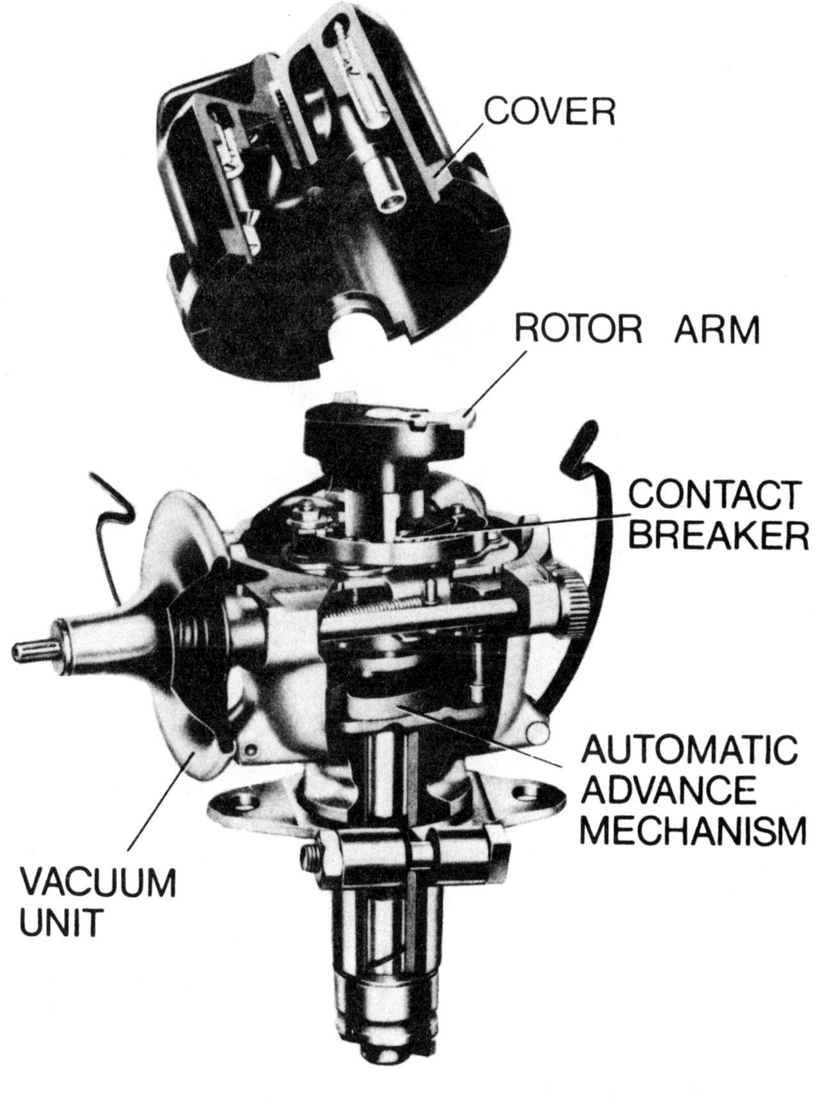

Fig. 3.1 - Typical Lucas distributor cutaway to show its internal parts.

The amounts by which both the automatic centrifugal advance mechanism and the vacuum control alter the spark timing are determined by the engine manufacturer by trial and error on a test bed with manual control of the ignition.

Fig. 3.2 - Rotation of the distributor cam opens and closes the contact breaker against a curved single-blade spring.

Since the centrifugal mechanism relies on very small tension springs attached to bob weights, it is susceptible to spring weakening or lack of lubrication.

Automatic Advance

Lucas distributors contain two steel weights under the base plate carrying the contact breaker, arranged to pivot outwards under centrifugal force, turning the hollow shaft above on which is machined the cam for the contact breaker. Two springs hold the mechanism in the static position by linking pegs on the cam foot to anchor posts on what is termed the action plate, the stiffness of these springs being chosen to control the rate of advance. As the weights are flung out by centrifugal force against the springs, the cam assembly turns in the direction

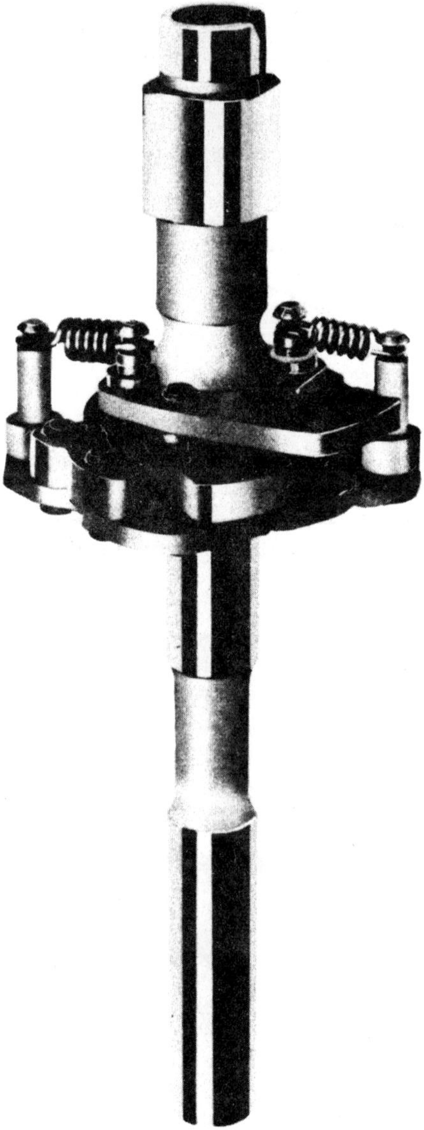

Fig. 3.3 - The bob weights for the auto advance mechanism are mounted on a base plate with small tension springs to counter the centrifugal forces. As the weights move out the cam above turns on the central shaft.

of rotation, thus causing the contacts to open earlier and the spark to advance its timing in the cycle of the engine. Usually, most of the advance is required in the low-to-medium speed range, so to prevent over advance at the top end, a stop is provided (by causing an extension of one weight to butt against one of the fixed anchor posts) to limit the movement of the cam assembly.

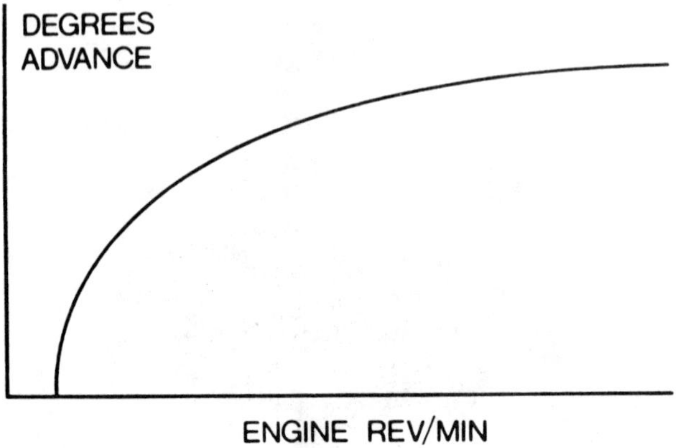

Fig. 3.4 - Typical engine advance curve showing how the timing should vary with speed.

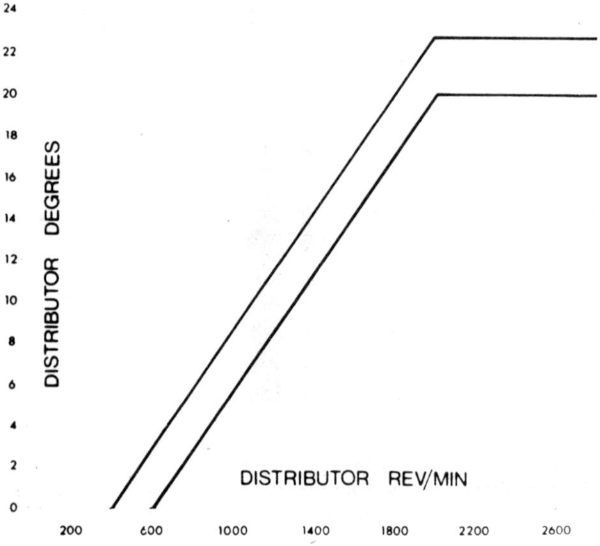

Fig. 3.5 - Actual advance curve with two equal stiffness distributor bob-weight springs. At about 1,900 rpm of the distributor shaft (3,800 engine rpm) the weights reach their stops.

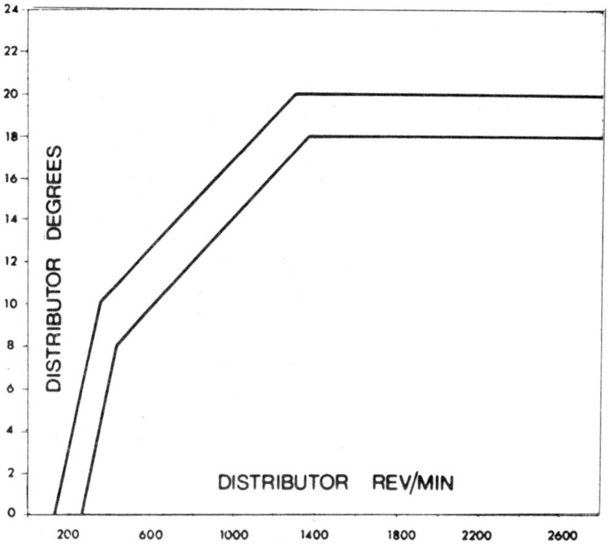

Fig. 3.6 - To obtain an advance curve closer to the ideal requirement, unequal springs are used with this effect.

Some distributors have a pair of identical springs, carefully matched, and these provide a linear advance curve as engine speed rises. Another type employs two different springs, one tight in the static position and the other initially slack, giving a two-stage effect to the advance curve produced, for more delicate control of the spark timing. The tight spring is relatively soft, giving a rapid initial advance up until the second, much stiffer spring takes effect, reducing the slope of the graph and slowing down the rate of advance.

When the engine is running lightly laden at high speed, even more advance of the timing is required to give good performance and fuel economy. Another way of looking at it is that under heavy load at low speed the spark must be retarded to prevent pinking or detonation. This latter setting is the normal one, but under light loads when induction depression is high the timing is advanced by the diaphragm and base plate linkage already mentioned. The vacuum assembly is marked with code numbers indicating its callibration, the first figure being the vacuum (in inches of mercury) at which the unit starts to function, the second being the vacuum at which the maximum advance occurs, and the last figure being the maximum advance in degrees of flywheel rotation.

Where a vernier adjustment is provided on the distributor it is integrated with the vacuum control, a small scale being marked on the vacuum diaphragm body where it emerges from the distributor. A knurled screw at the opposite end of the link to the base plate has a ratchet looking device and turning it gives very fine adjustment of the timing.

Fig. 3.7 - Counterweight mechanism of the distributor exposed to show its location in the base of the housing and its installation details. This unit has equal springs.

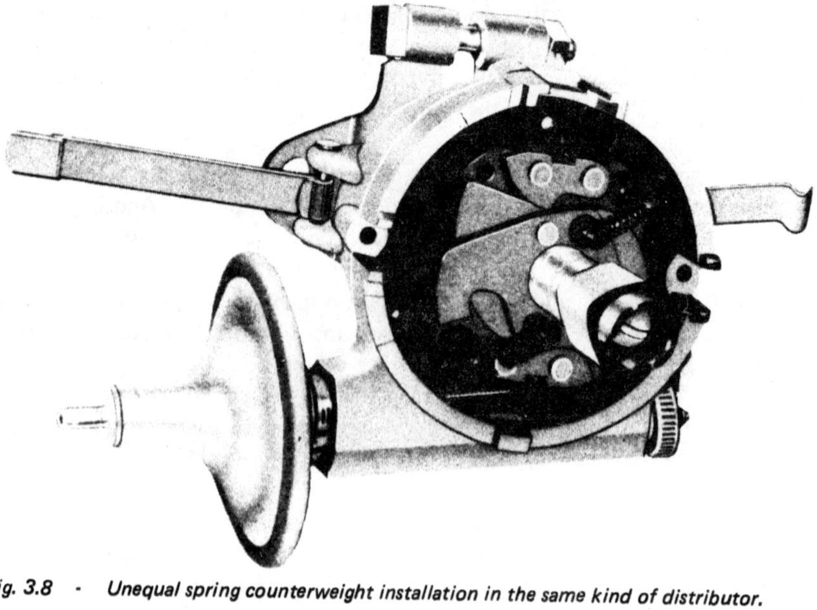

Fig. 3.8 - Unequal spring counterweight installation in the same kind of distributor.

Condensers

The purpose of the condenser or capacitor, which is usually mounted inside the distributor next to the contacts, is to bring about a more rapid collapse of the magnetic field in the coil and hence boost the secondary voltage induced. The capacitor itself comprises a roll of metallised paper inside a metal can, one side of the rolled strip being connected to a supply lead and the other to earth via a terminal on the can. The capacitance is about 0.20 microfarads and the overall size about 5/8in. diameter by about 1in.

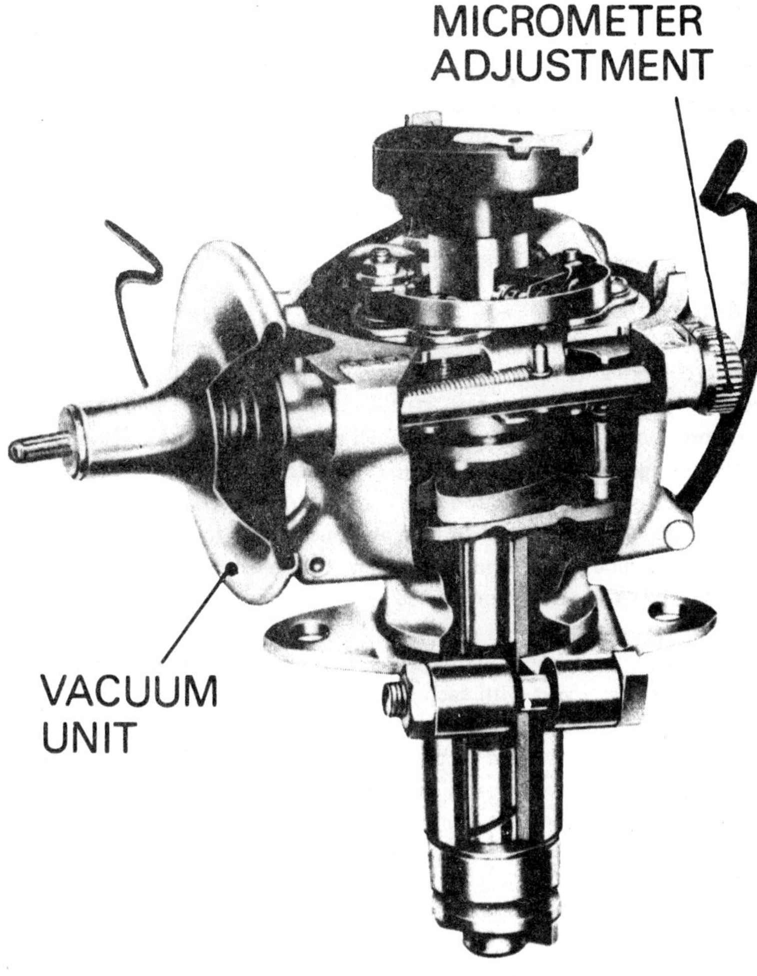

Fig. 3.9 - The micrometer adjustment, when fitted, is incorporated in the vacuum advance mechanism.

When the contact points open, the primary induced voltage switches to the alternative path through the capacitor rather than try to jump the opening gap and cause arcing. The current passing through the capacitor builds up an electrostatic charge until it reaches a higher potential than that in the rest of the primary circuit. It then discharges back through the coil and starts to be re-charged again in the same manner. The energy induced in the primary circuit is thus totally dissipated with relatively little damage to the contact breaker points.

There is still a small amount of arcing across the points nut not enough to cause trouble for at least 3,000 miles and often an engine can run for up to 6,000 miles without attention to the points. Without the capacitor in the circuit there would be much more rapid burning of the points as well as a considerably reduced secondary high-tension voltage output from the coil. Although modern capacitors are designed to be self-healing and their life is usually extremely long, failures do occur in service with immediate effects on the efficiency of the ignition system.

Rotor Arm and Distributor Cap

These two components take care of the high-tension distribution and they work independently of the low-tension part of the distributor already described. Supply from the coil enters the cap through a central electrode and passes down through a spring-loaded carbon brush to a brass contact moulded into the rotor arm. The rotor is mounted on top of the distributor shaft, usually being a light press fit on the end of the cam with an asymmetric dog to locate it correctly. It turns at half engine speed and directs the high-tension charge to whichever cylinder is near the top of its compression stroke.

In the distributor cap therefore is one electrode for each cylinder, a high-tension wire connecting it with each sparking plug. The electrodes are brass or aluminium and they are moulded into the cap, equidistant from each other and at a radius which places them as close as possible to the tip of the rotor as it turns. The bodies of the rotor and the cap are moulded in high-quality bakelite to prevent the charge taking any path other than that required, this phenomenon being known as tracking. As a film of damp on the outside can cause tracking (and hence misfiring of the engine), distributors in exposed positions are often fitted with a moulded plastic "boot", to keep out moisture.

Tracking can occur when there is a path offering less resistance than the smooth surface of the mouldings, a crack being a common example of just such a path.

Fig. 3.10 - Lucas distributor type 23D4, the simplest unit with centrifugal advance only.

As a temporary get-you-home measure cracks can be sprayed with an insulating lacquer, an ordinary ladies' hair spray being suitable in an emergency.

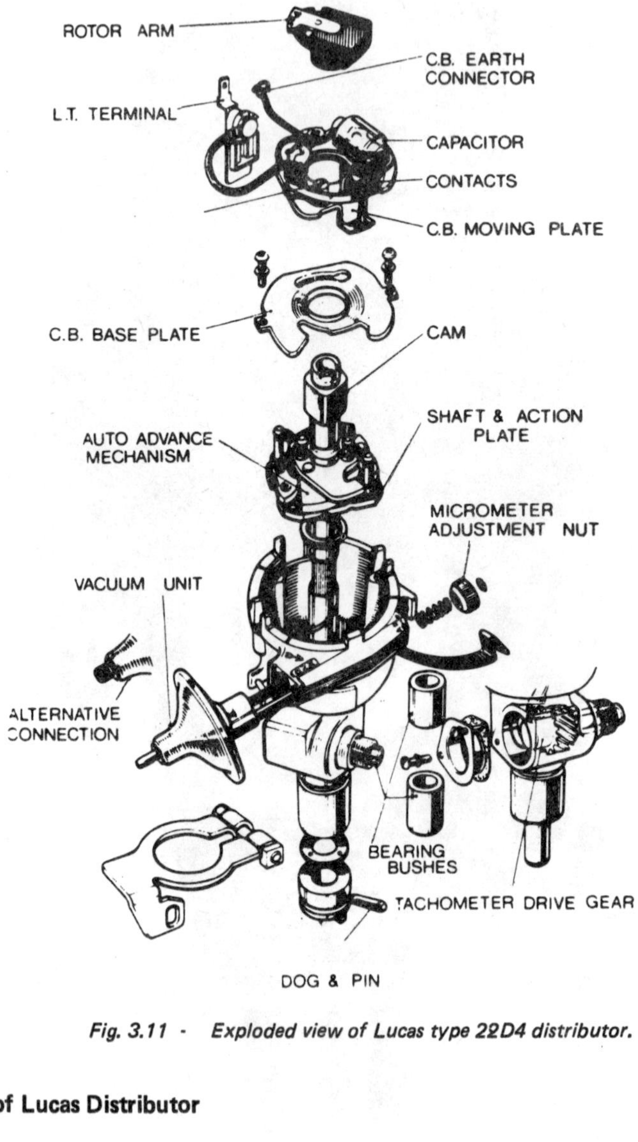

Fig. 3.11 - Exploded view of Lucas type 22D4 distributor.

Types of Lucas Distributor

There are three models of Lucas distributor in use on modern cars, the 22D, 23D and 25D, the type code being followed by a number representing how many cylinders are in the engine. Vertical caps with screw-in terminals for the high-tension leads are now practically obsolete, and the horizontal type of cap with grub screw connections which gripped and pierced the leads is only used in a few applications. The most common type of cap has push-in connections, crimped terminals on the leads being a tight fit in the moulded chimneys.

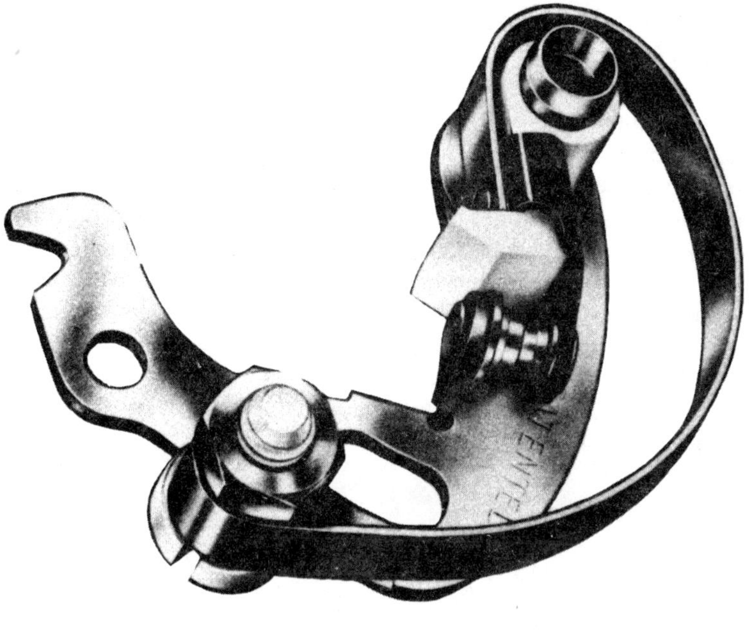

Fig. 3.12 - One-piece contact point assembly.

The majority of cars use the 25D distributor which is available for either 4- or 6-cylinder engines. This unit has an aluminium body with the vacuum unit built in and a vernier control provided for fine timing adjustment. Bearing bushes for the distributor shaft are oil impregnated before assembly and they receive additional lubrication by oil mist from the engine. The four-cylinder version has copper/iron bushes which can be replaced, while the six-cylinder version has sintered iron bushes machined to close tolerances making replacement impractical.

A longer version of the 25D known as the 22D contains two sintered iron bushes with improved bearing surfaces and a reduced possibility of play developing. This controls the timing more accurately. The 22D will be found on either

4- or 6-cylinder engines and it may or may not have a vacuum control and vernier adjustment.

A simpler version of the 25D without vacuum control or vernier is known as the 23D. It is not fitted to many cars since it controls the timing only by centrifugal means.

Replacing Contact Sets

Most replacement sets are now in the form of a one-piece assembly, reducing the chance of incorrect installation and improving the contact alignment. There is now much less likelihood of small nuts, washers or insulating bushes being dropped and lost, and the task of replacing contacts is much simplified. It is now a relatively easy job to undo the clamping screw, lift off the old set, insert the new assembly and retighten the clamping screw lightly. With the heel of the cam follower resting on a peak of the cam, set the contact gap to the specified open distance with a feeler gauge or adjust the dwell angle with a meter if available. Tighten the clamping screw securely and recheck the gap or dwell angle. It is now essential to retime the ignition, preferably with a strobe lamp (see Chapter 7).

Chaper 4

Leads and Spark Plugs

Without suppression, the ignition system of the car would interfere with domestic radio and television as well as a radio fitted in the car, so it is provided to a limited degree in the standard equipment. Usually this takes the form of the minimum required to prevent domestic interference, and additional suppression may be required when fitting a car radio.

Generally the most common way of providing suppression is the use of resistive plug leads. These are made of graphite impregnated rayon braiding, covered in pvc insulation. Two grades are available with resistances of 4,000-7,000 ohm/ft and 7,000-10,000 ohm/ft, the object being to give all leads the same total resistance regardless of their length. For the resistance to be effective a minimum of 5,000 ohm is required and ideally about 12,500 ohm is best.

It is a common fallacy that resistive leads reduce the intensity of the spark at the plug. This is not true and the only noticeable effects of replacing resistive leads with plain ones on some engines would be slightly easier starting and more even running at a low-speed (less than 600 rpm) idle.

To suppress the low-tension circuit of the ignition and reduce interference on a car radio, a 1 microfarad capacitor is usually connected between the SW (+) terminal of the coil and a good earth such as the coil mounting bracket.

For a spark plug to give its best the temperature of the electrodes should be in the region of 500-600 deg C. If it runs hotter than this there is a danger of pre-ignition, and if it runs cooler there may be fouling from carbon deposits. All engines are different and the grade of plug is carefully chosen by the designer to run at the right temperature. Usually the length of the central electrode and the mass of metal surrounding it vary with the grade of plug. The wrong grade of plug in an engine can cause not only misfiring but serious damage like burnt valves and even holed pistons.

Before carrying out any work on the ignition system therefore, it is essential to check that the plugs are to the correct specification, clean and set to the right gap.

The voltage required for the plug to spark varies with the nature of running from around 5,000 volts at normal loads and temperatures to as high as 12,000 volts in a slightly fouled condition. For smooth running at all times it is normal for the coil to provide a voltage well in excess of the plug requirement. Any deficiency in the system which reduces the coil output usually shows up under full load driving when the plug voltage requirement is greatest.

Chapter 5

High Performance Engines

Where an engine has been designed or tuned to develop the utmost power possible, precise control of the ignition timing is vital. Such unwanted factors as play in the distributor shaft, high resistance in the contact faces or insufficient secondary voltage to fire the mixture with partially fouled spark plugs under load reduce the normally high engine efficiency and cause a loss of performance.

Many modern engines now produce specific power outputs that exceed those of the racing cars a few years ago, and these engines require ignition timing to very close tolerances, especially if they are high revving.

A normal single contact breaker for a 4-cylinder engine has a dwell angle of about 60 deg and in order for sufficient voltage to build up in the primary ignition circuit, the minimum time the contacts must remain together is about 2 milliseconds. This means a practical rev limit of 8,400 rpm for a four-cylinder engine and 5,600 rpm for a six, which has a dwell angle of only 30 deg. With eight cylinders the rev limit should be only 4,200 rpm which is why most vee-8 engines have two contact breakers sharing the task inside one distributor. With a high-revving vee-12 there is sometimes a pair of distributors or, in the case of the Jaguar V12 unit, electronic assistance to help speed up the process.

Obviously the time the points remain closed is totally dependent upon the dwell angle or gap setting between them. Every possible care should be taken when setting this gap, as any maladjustment will seriously affect the high-speed performance. Similarly, any play in the distributor shaft or wear of the fibre or nylon cam follower will upset the ignition by altering both the dwell angle and the exact timing of the spark. If the cam follower wears, the timing is retarded and the dwell angle increased outside the prescribed limits. So critical is the contact breaker setting on some engines that a feeler gauge is no longer good enough and some form of electric dwell meter which physically measures the angle of cam rotation during which current actually passes through the contacts, preferably with the engine running to eliminate any backlash effects in the distributor drive, is almost a necessity.

Generally speaking, as long as the distributor is in good condition it should be able to cope with a hotted-up engine without any attention other than routine maintenance. First check that there is no play in the main shaft and that the rotor arm is a snug fit on the end of the cam. If there are any signs of excessive movement when you try to wriggle the rotor sideways, remove the whole distributor assembly and check the bottom end of the shaft. With the Lucas type 25D4 it is possible to replace the impregnated copper/iron bushes, but on the 25D6 you must exchange the whole assembly under the B90 scheme.

Another factor which can seriously reduce performance is stickiness in the centrifugal advance mechanism and this should be checked, in the absence of any proper electronic equipment, by turning the rotor arm against its springs and feeling for the appropriate return action. Careful and sparing lubrication of the bob-weight pivots and a light application of oil under the rotor arm is advisable at regular intervals, and to prevent rapid cam follower wear the face should be wiped with a hard retentive grease such as Retinax A.

When fitting a new contact set it is worth bearing in mind that there will be some initial bedding down of the cam follower and this will retard the timing slightly and close up the gap. The process is usually complete within 500 miles driving, after which gap and timing should be reset. If any competition work is envisaged, make sure this process has taken place well before the event starts.

Optimum timing and the dangers of over-advance

Usually the manufacturer's recommendations on ignition timing represent the best setting for all conditions, but when searching for the ultimate on a particular engine it may be advantageous to deviate slightly. The quoted figure has to cover a wide span of production tolerances and there may be a good reason why your engine needs timing slightly in advance or retard of the figure in the book. In the days when timing was far less critical it was good enough to simply rotate the distributor back and forth with the engine running until the maximum idling speed was obtained.

A much more satisfactory way is to experiment on the road, timing the car under load over a wide speed range - like from 30 to 70 mph in top - until the optimum is obtained. An alternative method is to find a long steady gradient and at a marked point near the bottom apply full throttle in top from a fixed speed - say 30 mph - and note the speed as the car passes a marker further on near the top. Only very small changes should be made each time, both in advance of the standard setting and retarded from it. Never make any other adjustment at the same time or all the results will be invalid. All this time and trouble is rarely worth the effort as in most cases you will only confirm that the manufacturer's setting is the best.

If you have made modifications to the engine, like raising the compression ratio or improving the breathing by fitting new manifolds and different carburetters, such experimenting may pay handsome dividends. By modifying the engine in this way you are greatly increasing the load on the ignition system and are much more likely to run into misfiring problems since the voltage required at the plug electrodes to give a spark increases in direct proportion to the compression pressure in the spark plug gap. Any sooty deposits which cool the electrodes also increase the voltage requirement, which is why an engine often misfires when it's first given full throttle after a long spell of gentle driving in town. Less voltage is required if the centre electrode, which runs hotter than the one attached to the threaded surround, has negative polarity because when it gets very hot it emits electrons which assist the spark (the high-tension voltage is a back emf remember, so the spark jumps from negative pole to positive one). Some engines rely on this phenomenon at high revs and if, for any reason the polarity of the primary circuit is reversed at the coil, misfiring may occur. All Lucas coils are wound so that the direction of the secondary voltage causes the centre plug electrode to have a negative polarity regardless of the car's battery polarity, the engine completing the circuit with positive high-tension polarity. If the coil is marked with a "+" and a "-" sign on its low-tension primary connections, it is impossible to go wrong. If it is of the type marked SW and CB it has different internal connections depending on whether it was intended for a vehicle with positive or negative earth. Almost all cars now are designed for negative earth, so the problem is one of increasing rarity.

When making alterations to the standard ignition setting beware of over advancing the timing. Low-speed full throttle detonation or audible "pinking" is distinctive and should be avoided by retarding the timing or using a better grade of fuel. A much more serious phenomenon is high-speed pre-ignition which is not audible and can cause burnt valves or a piston failure very rapidly. It occurs when the octane requirement of the engine exceeds that of the fuel, and an over-advanced ignition can be a likely cause. When taking a high performance car abroad to a country where 100 octane fuel is not available it is advisable to retard the timing from the normal setting to prevent pre-ignition.

Chapter 6

Transistor Assisted System

With the common availability of semiconductors like transistors which behave as an electronic switch without moving parts, the ignition system became a natural application of these clever devices. With the aid of a transistorised circuit the current passing through the contacts is reduced to a very small value reducing the arcing and extending the contact life drastically. As there is negligible arcing the magnetic field in the primary winding of the coil collapses more rapidly, improving the sparking voltage especially at low speed and in cold temperatures. The advantages of transistor assisted systems are therefore mostly by way of reduced contact maintenance, the normal interval between adjustments being 25,000 miles. Easier starting in difficult conditions is an additional benefit, plus a boosted high-tension voltage from the coil which helps spark the plug when conditions in the combustion chamber are difficult. A transistor ignition system is not a magical way to boost engine performance; it simply keeps the equipment in peak condition for longer.

Without going into the involved atomic theory that causes a semiconductor sandwich to act as an electronic switch, it is relatively easy ro understand that by applying a low current to the base layer the resistance between the other two layers reduces immediately making it, in effect, like a closed switch in the "on" position. Breaking the circuit supplying the base restores a high resistance between the other two layers, opening the "switch" without the associated problems of mechanical movement and of a high load being interrupted.

In applying this aid to the ignition system it is usual to retain the contact breaker in the distributor as the low current triggering device, removing the capacitor, and substitute a new high-performance coil with ballast resistor to limit the voltage applied to it and prevent over-heating. A transistor unit containing a printed circuit wiring board and all the necessary electronic components mounted in an aluminium heat sink completes the set which is designed for easy installation in cars with conventional ignition systems.

Lucas manufacture two kits, both called T.A.C.4, one for negative earth cars and the other for positive earth installations. The negative earth system is the more complex because additional circuitry and an extra transistor are required to trigger the power transistor. Those who understand electric circuits will be

Fig. 6.1 - Lucas transistor assisted contact kit, available as an accessory.

able to follow the workings of the two Lucas systems shown in the diagram. Those who do not follow what is happening would do best to stick closely to the fitting instructions when making a transistor ignition installation and not bother with the full working details.

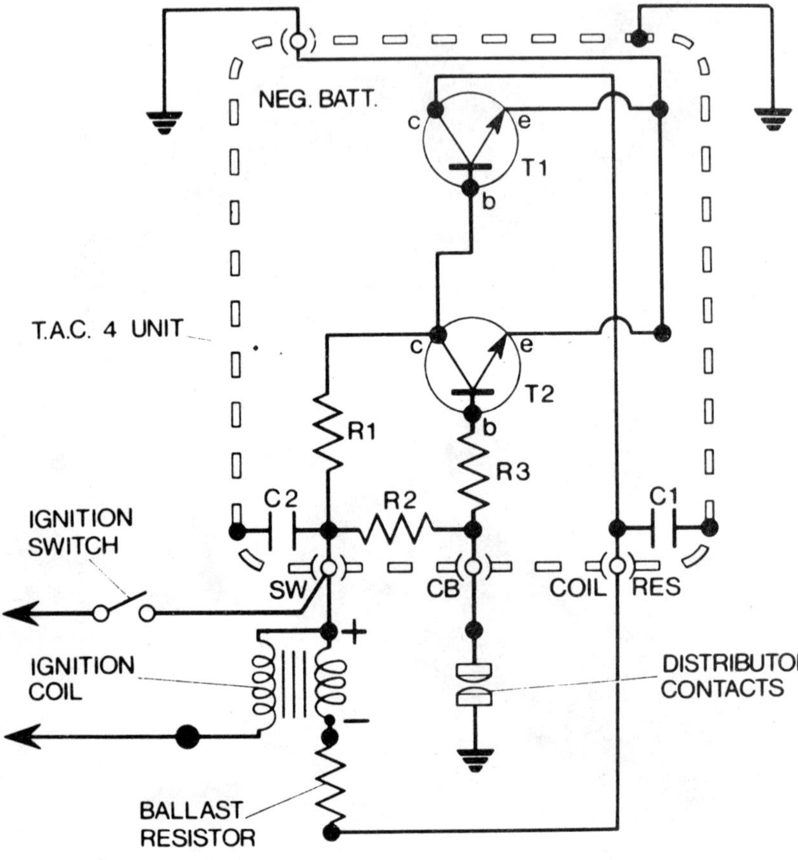

Fig. 6.2 - Transistor assisted ignition circuit for a typical negative earth installation.

In fact, the functioning of the circuit is very simple. With a positive earth car, when the contacts close a small current is allowed to flow through a control resistance and the base of the transistor, switching what is termed the collector/emitter junction into the "on" low-resistance condition. When this happens a larger current is allowed to flow from the battery through the primary winding of the coil via the ballast resistor. When the contacts open, the circuit for the base of the transistor is broken and the transistor immediately becomes non-conductive across its collector/emitter junction, interrupting the current flowing through the primary circuit of the coil and causing the magnetic field to collapse rapidly. This induces a back emf in the secondary windings in the same way as with a conventional ignition system.

With a negative earth installation extra resistors and a second transistor are added to trigger the power transistor since semiconductors are very directional devices which cannot have their polarity reversed. Both systems have a capacitor built in to suppress radio interference and a second capacitor to protect the transistor from high voltage surges.

Chapter 7

Use of the Strobe Lamp

Whilst a skilled mechanic can make a good job of timing the ignition of an engine statically, there is no real substitute for doing it with the engine running and there is no way the automatic and vacuum advance characteristics can be checked without some form of test equipment, the simplest and cheapest aid being a stroboscopic lamp. These can be either mains powered or energised by the ignition system itself, the latter producing a relatively weak beam which is difficult to see clearly in sunshine or bright daylight. The self-energising type is much cheaper however and just as effective in what it does.

Essentially a strobe lamp is a small hand torch with a neon tube as the light source. The speed at which the light flashes can be varied (on some devices it is used to measure revs) but for use with the ignition systems the rate must be equal to, or a simple multiple of, the crankshaft speed. The usual thing is to arrange for the high-tension voltage to Number 1 cylinder to trigger the neon tube.

As the lamp only flashes when Number 1 cylinder is firing, it will "freeze" the image of the timing mark on the flywheel or front pulley and show its position with the engine running in relation to the pointer provided. Thus the distributor can be rotated or the micrometer adjustment used to line up the two marks perfectly. A Blob of white paint or a chalk mark on the timing notches and pointer helps show them up in the strobe lamp beam.

In addition to timing the ignition at idling speed the strobe lamp can be used to check the automatic centrifugal advance, provided the specified values are known (see Appendix II) and the appropriate marks made on the pulley, flywheel or pointer support. As the engine speed is increased the mark on the pulley or flywheel will advance in the opposite direction to rotation as the spark occurs earlier. With the vacuum pipe disconnected from the distributor, the centrifugal advance can be checked. The exact amount of the vacuum advance cannot be checked by this primative means, but whether or not it is working at all will be seen if the throttle is blipped with the pipe reconnected. For the vacuum advance mechanism to work fully the engine must be at high revs on a small throttle opening - conditions for maximum induction vacuum. If the mark on the pulley moves to the same position it reached without the vacuum connection, and no further, when the throttle is blipped, the vacuum advance is inoperative for some reason. If it moves momentarily, the mechanism is probably functioning correctly. Faults in the vacuum system are mostly of the sort which make it fail completely, so this check is a useful one.

Most engines are provided with only the basic static timing marks in the form of one or two notches on the crankshaft pulley. With maximum total advance of the order of 30 deg, additional marks will be needed for these checks. Some of the strobe lamps available come complete with a protractor for marking out the pully rim, but even if this is missing it is a simple job to make scribe lines (much easier with the engine out on a bench, so think of this during a rebuild) and then convert the ends to painted marks so that they can be seen easily in the strobe beam. Accuracy is all important here, so take the time and trouble to make a proper job of it.

Chapter 8

Troubleshooting

Basically there are two kinds of ignition fault, the sort which stops the engine or prevents it from starting and the kind which causes poor running and loss of efficiency. The first part of this chapter will be devoted to the checks one should perform on a car which has stopped or has failed to start. The second part will cover ways of detecting and rectifying the latter kind of fault.

1. Engine Fails to Start

If the battery is in sound condition and the starter action vigorous, first remove a spraking plug and examine the condition of the electrodes. Make sure the gap is correct and the surfaces clear of carbon build-up or whiskery deposits. If the plug is wet with neat petrol there may be a carburetter fault, although if the ignition is healthy there should be some signs of at least one cylinder firing during the attempted starting.

With clean and correctly set plugs, the easiest check to make next is at the distributor contacts. Switch the ignition on and flick them open. There should be a spark here if the low tension circuit is sound. If there is a spark here, next remove the high-tension lead from the centre of the distributor cap and hold it about ¼in. from a good earth, such as the block or one of the head holding-down studs. Flick the distributor contacts again and watch for a spark jumping across from the end of the high-tension lead to earth. If there is a spark the fault is in the rotor arm and visible tracking marks should be obvious. If a spark is not obtained, the secondary coil winding is faulty. Whilst flicking the distributor contacts, feel to make sure the pivot moves freely and the points are not jammed open.

In the event of there being no spark at the distributor contacts when flicked with the ignition switched on, the fault is in the primary low-tension circuit, which should be checked thoroughly from the battery right through. If at any point in the following progressive check a zero voltage reading is obtained, the fault lies in the part of the circuit immediately "upstream" of the connection being checked. For these basic continuity checks a test lamp with two leads will do instead of a voltmeter, but for proper efficiency checks a voltmeter is essential.

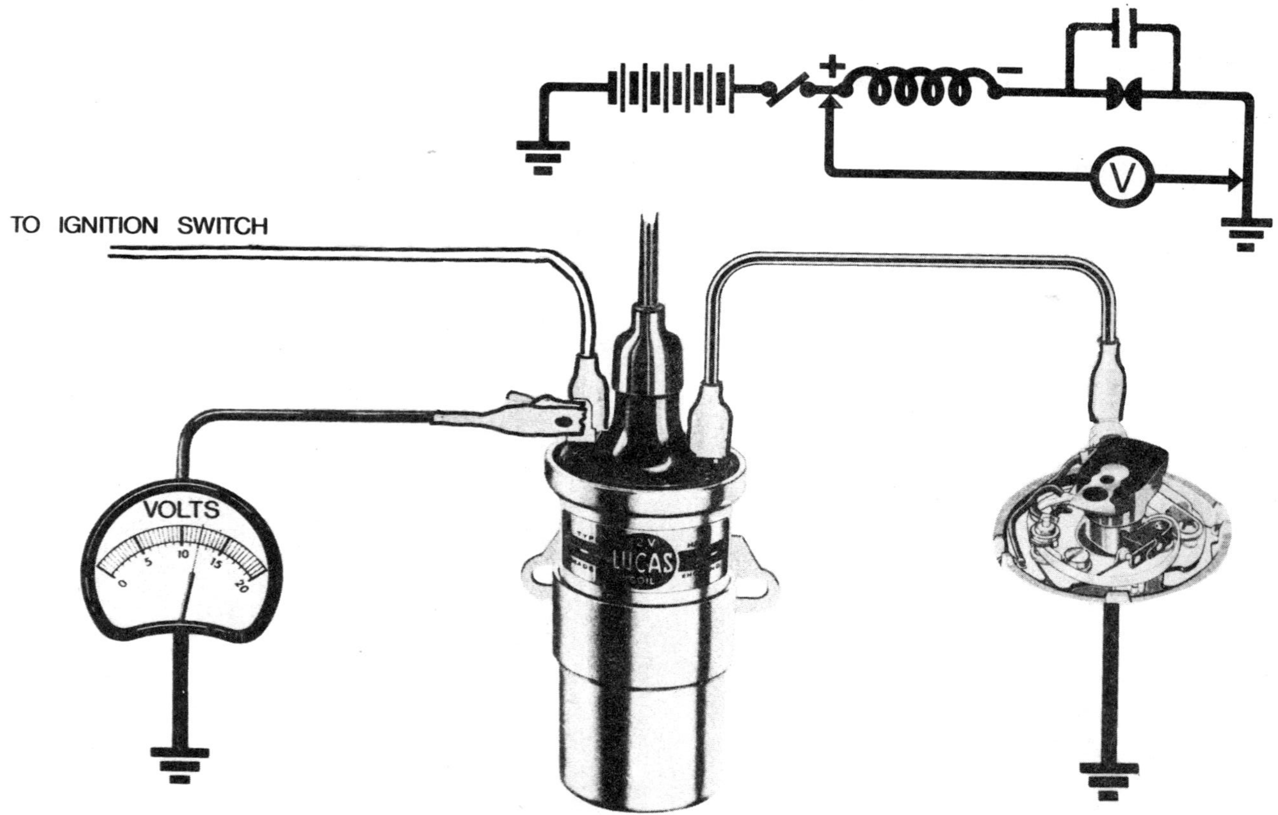

Fig. 8.1 - Checking the primary circuit with a voltmeter at the positive terminal of the coil. Distributor contacts closed.

First connect voltmeter or test lamp between the SW or "+" terminal of the coil and a good earth. Switch on the ignition; although it does not matter at this stage, it is better if the distributor contacts are closed. If the voltmeter indicates battery voltage or a 12-volt test bulb glows brightly, the supply to the coil is OK.

If there is no voltmeter reading or the test lamp fails to light, there is an open circuit between the control box and the coil, most likely at the ignition switch (check for whether accessories working through the ignition, e.g. wipers, heater fan, etc., are functioning).

Next check the primary coil winding for continuity, making sure that the contacts are open for this test. Move the coil test connection from the SW or "+" terminal to the CB or "-" one. If there is zero voltage to earth or the lamp fails to glow there is either a break in the primary coil winding or a short to earth in the distributor. Remove the lead from the CB or "-" terminal; if the voltmeter then reads battery voltage or the lamp suddenly lights, there is a short in the distributor. If not, the primary coil winding has a break in it.

Should this test reveal a short in the distributor, check first that the low-tension lead from the coil to the distributor is sound. If this is sound and is making good connections at both ends, inspect the insulation of the flexible lead connecting the low-tension terminal on the distributor to the moving contact and that from the same terminal to the condenser. If there are both in good condition, make sure that there is an insulating washer under the moving contact. Finally check that the condenser is not earthed (other than by its casing) and that the tags on the condenser lead and the flexible lead from the low-tension terminal are under the nylon bush and not the nut securing the bush.

Next, with the voltmeter or test lamp still connected between the CB or "-" terminal of the coil and earth, close the distributor contacts by turning the engine slightly. If there is any voltage shown or the test bulb glows even slightly there is dirt, oil or damp on the contacts, the setting is not correct and they cannot close properly or the earth connections are poor. The flexible lead from the contact plate to earth should be checked as well as the mating surface between the distributor and the engine block.

2. Engine Runs Badly, Uses Too Much Fuel or Misfires

This kind of behaviour indicates that the spark is either too weak or it is occuring at the wrong time. Weak sparks are caused by insufficient voltage at the plug, too high a resistance between the electrodes (gap too wide or plug fouled

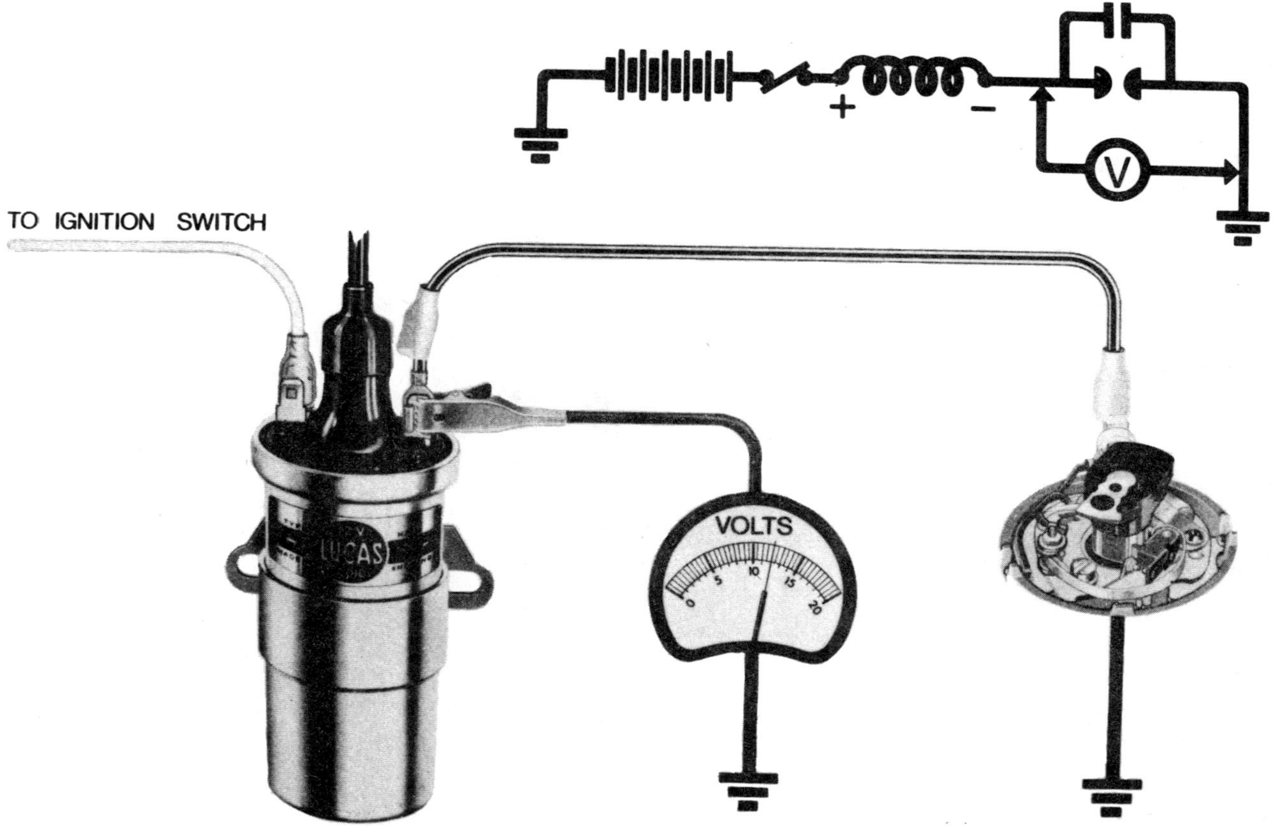

Fig. 8.2 - Checking the primary circuit with a voltmeter at the negative terminal of the coil. Distributor contacts open.

with deposits) or shorting to earth. If the plugs are in good order, first check the points in the distributor. A faulty condenser will cause rapid pitting of their faces and a weak spark. Check by substituting one known to be in good condition (e.g. from another car); the visible spark between a high-tension lead from the coil to earth should noticeably improve with the good condenser if the normal one is faulty.

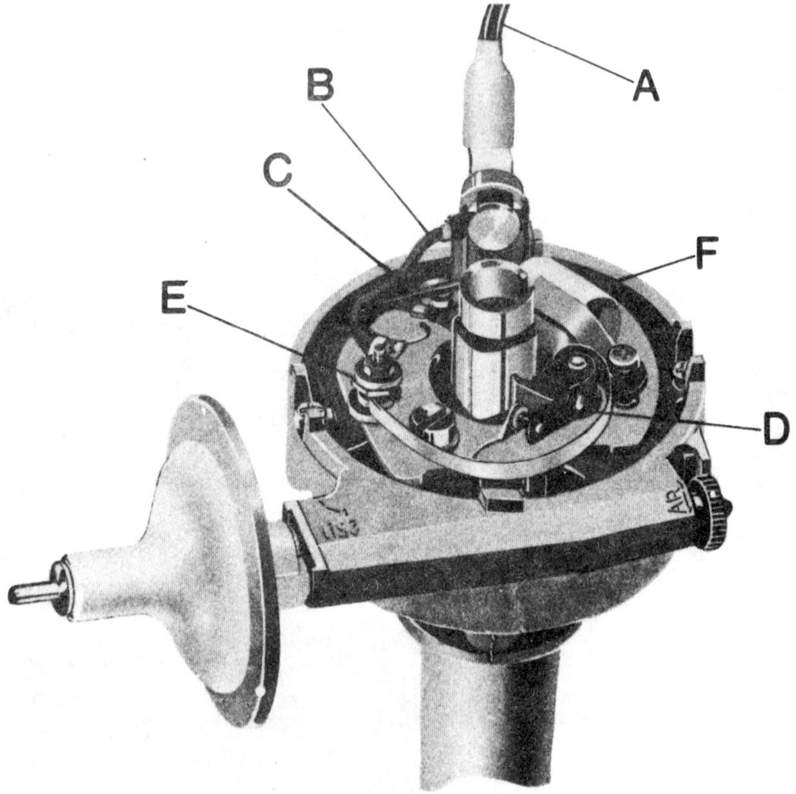

Fig. 8.3 - Points to check when a distributor earthing failure is suspected. (A) Low-tension lead between coil and distributor. (B) Flexible lead connecting main low-tension terminal to the moving contact. (C) Flexible lead connecting contact breaker terminal post to the capacitor. (D) Check spring is not touching angle plate. (E) Check soldered tags are under nylon bush on terminal post and not under nut. (F) Disconnect capacitor to check that it is not shorting internally.

Tracking either in the distributor or along the insulation of a high-tension lead can be caused by moisture which has condensed after a night in the open or by

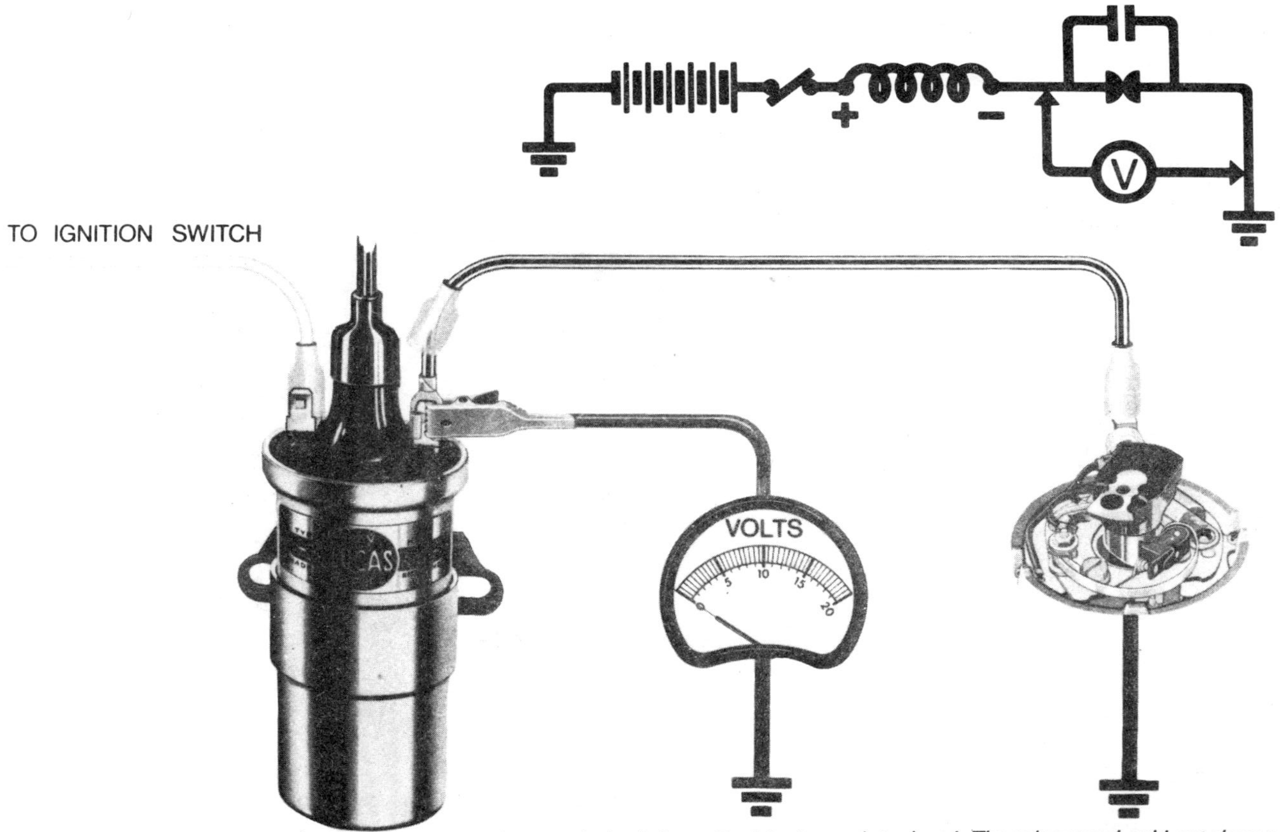

Fig. 8.4 - Checking the primary voltage at the negative terminal of the coil with the points closed. The voltmeter should not show a reading.

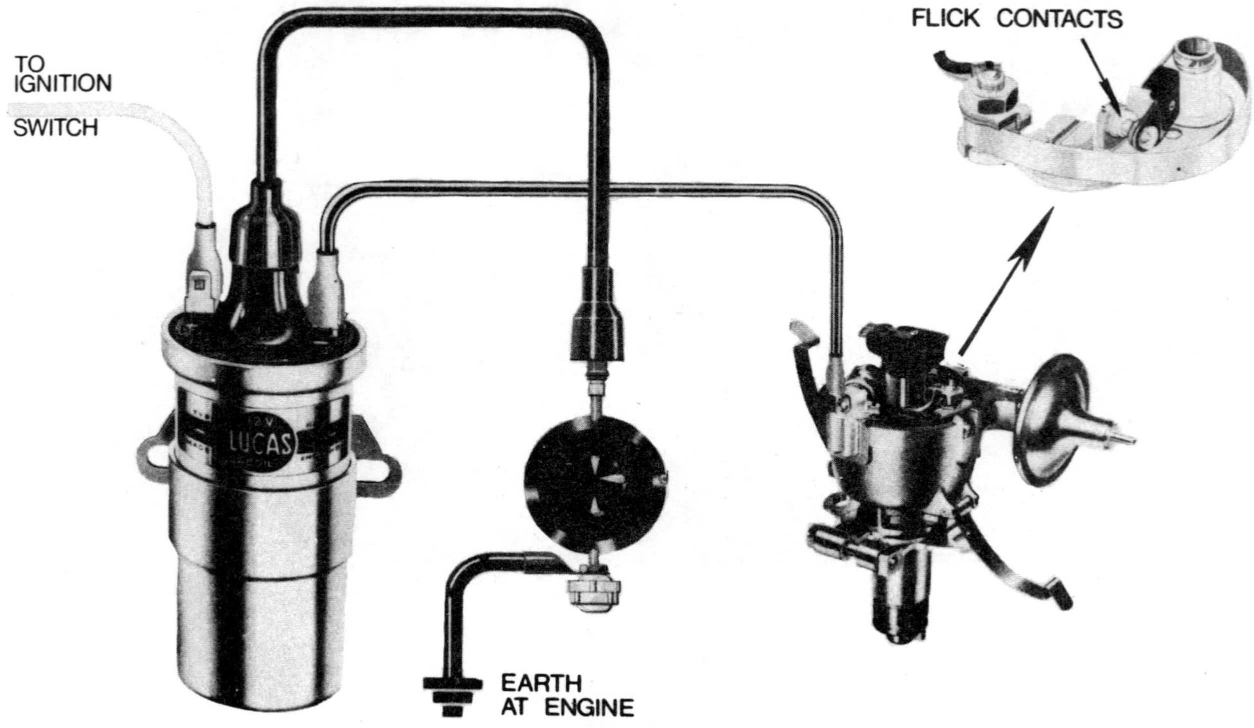

Fig, 8.5 *With a three-point spark gap or by holding the coil HT lead near an earth (e.g. the engine block), flick the contacts to check the secondary circuit.*

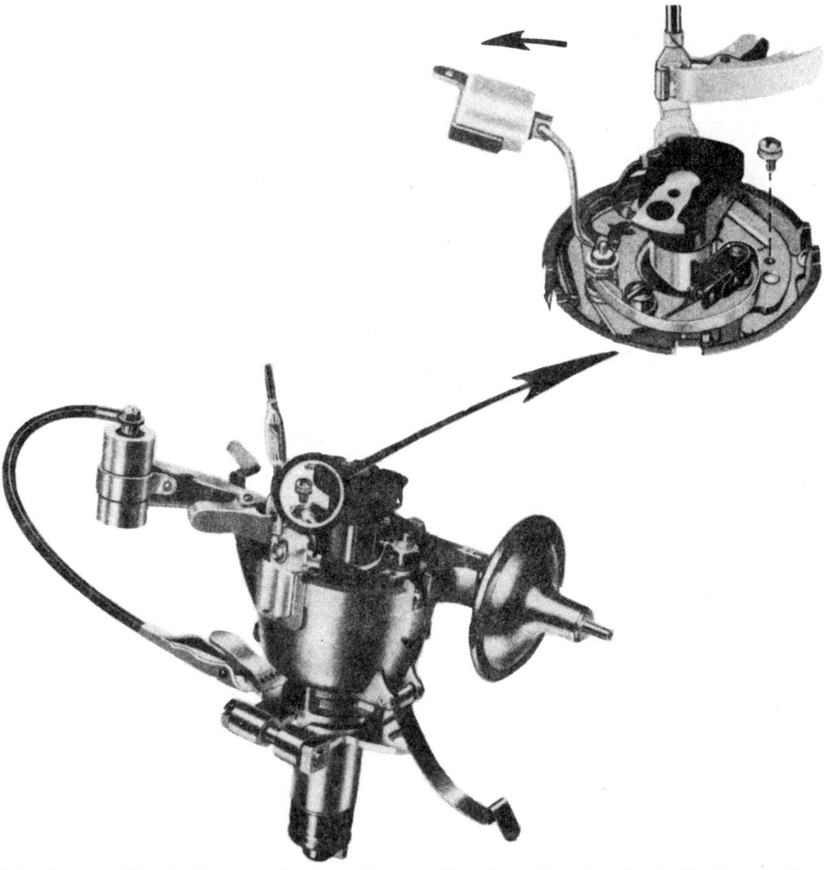

Fig. 8.6 - Check the capacitor by disconnecting the original and substituting another which is known to be in good condition.

spray during heavy rain. Tracking paths on the rotor arm or inside the distributor cap can be seen as cracks; a temporary get-you-home trick is to spray the area with ordinary ladies' hair lacquer. Damp can be expelled with one of the proprietry aerosols such as Holts Damp-Start, Combat or WD 40. As a first check always make sure the rotor arm rotates freely against the centrifugal springs and returns of its own accord. A more thorough check is to measure the maximum advance (with the vacuum connection, if fitted, removed) with a strobe lamp. Most ignition faults are caused by dirty or corroded connections or neglect of the contact breaker. When cleaning and resetting the contact breaker gap, always retime the ignition. Generally speaking an over-retarded ignition causes poor fuel consumption, loss of power and possibly over-heating. Over-advanced ignition causes pinking and a similar loss of power, especially at high revs.

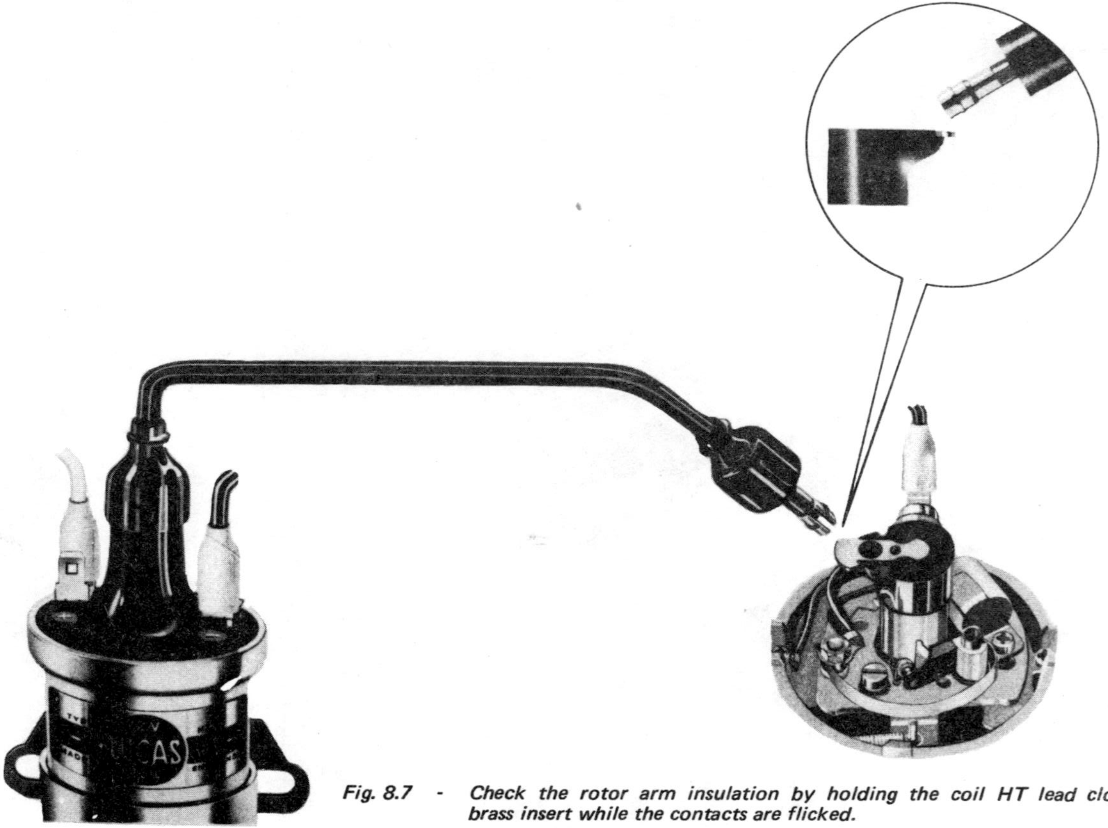

Fig. 8.7 - Check the rotor arm insulation by holding the coil HT lead close to the brass insert while the contacts are flicked.

APPENDIX

Test Data for Distributors

Distributors are listed in numerical sequence according to service reference number. Suffix letters are recorded only when they indicate an alteration to the test data. The test data recorded under suffix 'A' are therefore correct for all suffix letters unless a further letter is indicated. Part 'A' of this section contains the centrifugal advance test data for distributors.

CONTACT BREAKER

The contact breaker gap should be set and maintained at 0.014"-0.016" (0.36-0.41 mm). Some very old units may still be fitted with symmetric or asymmetric cams. This can be ascertained by inspection. The correct gap for these types is as follows:

Initial Setting	Service Setting (after 500 miles)
0.014"-0.016"	0.010"-0.012"
(0.36-0.41 mm)	(0.25-0.3 mm)

The gap should be checked by rotating the distributor shaft until a point of maximum opening is achieved, and then inserting an appropriate feeler gauge.

CAPACITOR

The most efficient way of checking the capacitor is by substitution. An open circuit capacitor will be indicated by excessive burning at the contacts.

A short circuit capacitor will be indicated by no interruption of the primary current when the contacts are closed.

Insulation resistance should be a minimum of 10 megohms at 500 volts D.C. However, it should be noted that only if the insulation resistance has fallen to an exceptionally low value will the performance be affected, that is, less than 3 megohms.

Capacity:

All distributors except model 18D2 ... ... 0.18–0.23 microfarad
Model 18D2 ... ... 0.14–0.20 microfarad
All contact breaker units except model 18D1 ... ...
... ... 0.18–0.23 microfarad
Model 18 D1 ... ... 0.14–0.20 microfarad

CONTACT BREAKER SPRING LOAD

The contact breaker spring load should be measured at the contacts.

All distributor and C.B. units except model 15D1 ... ...
... ... 18–24 ozf (5-6.7 N)
Model 15D1 ... ... 14–20 ozf (3.9-5.6 N)

CLAMP PLATE ASSEMBLY

Overtightening of the securing plate must be avoided. The maximum torque figures according to the type of assembly are as follows:

Trapped Nut Assembly ... ... 50 lbf in. (5.649 Nm.)
Trapped Bolt Assembly ... ... 30 lbf in. (3.389 Nm.)

CAM ANGLES

High lift cams – Contact Breaker Gap set to 0.015" + 0.001" (0.38 mm + 0.03 mm).

4 CYLINDER		6 CYLINDER		8 CYLINDER	
Open Period	Closed Period	Open Period	Closed Period	Open Period	Closed Period
$30^{o} \pm 3^{o}$	$60^{o} \pm 3^{o}$	$25^{o} \pm 3^{o}$	$35^{o} \pm 3^{o}$	$11^{o} \pm 3^{o}$	$34^{o} \pm 3^{o}$

Symmetric Cams – Contact Breaker Gap set to 0.011" + 0.001" (0.28 mm + 0.03 mm).

4 CYLINDER		6 CYLINDER		8 CYLINDER	
Open Period	Closed Period	Open Period	Closed Period	Open Period	Closed Period
$45^{o} \pm 4^{o}$	$45^{o} \pm 4^{o}$	$22^{o} \pm 4^{o}$	$38^{o} \pm 4^{o}$	$13^{o} \pm 2^{o}$	$32^{o} \pm 2^{o}$

Asymmetric Cams – Contact Breaker Gap set to 0.011" + 0.001" (0.28mm + 0.03 mm).

4 CYLINDER		6 CYLINDER		8 CYLINDER	
Open Period	Closed Period	Open Period	Closed Period	Open Period	Closed Period
$41^{\circ} \pm 4^{\circ}$	$49^{\circ} \pm 4^{\circ}$	–	–	–	–

FIRING ANGLES

4 CYLINDER	6 CYLINDER	8 CYLINDER
0°, 90°, 180°, $270^{\circ} \pm 1^{\circ}$	0°, 60°, 120°, etc. $\pm 1^{\circ}$	0°, 45°, 90°, etc. $\pm 1^{\circ}$

Service No.	Model	Rotation	Run up to (Rev/ Min)	Advance to be (Degrees)	Intermediate Advance I (Rev/ Min)	I (Degrees)	II (Rev/ Min)	II (Degrees)	No advance Below (Rev/ Min)
40033A	**DZ6A**	C.	2200	11.5-13.5	1100	5-7.5	700	1-3.5	300
40033B	**DVZ6A**	C.	2200	11.5-13.5	1100	5-7.5	700	1-3.5	300
40037A	**DZW4A**	C.	2500	9-11	1150	7-8.5	400	1-6	200
40037B	**DZS4A**	C.	2500	9-11	1150	7-8.5	400	1-6	200
40042A	**DKYH4A**	A/C.	2600	16-18	1550	13-15	800	7-11	300
40042B	**DKZH4A**	A/C.	2600	16-18	1550	13-15	800	7-11	300
40051A	**DY6A**	C.	1800	13-15	1200	10-12.5	600	2-4	200
40056A	**DKZH4A**	C.	2500	9-11	1800	9-10.5	400	1-6	200
40056B	**DKYH4A**	C.	2400	9-11	1600	8.5-9.5	400	1-6	200
40056D	**DKYH4A**	C.	2800	9-11	1800	9-10.5	400	1-6	200
40056E	**DKYH4A**	C.	2700	9-11	1750	8-10	450	0.5-2.5	200
40070A	**DKYH4A**	A/C.	2000	9-11	1400	8-10.5	700	1-3.5	300
40100A	**DKH4A**	A/C.	2500	13-15	1200	7-9	600	2-4	200
40116D	**DVZH6A**	C.	1500	14-16	470	6-8	300	1-5	100
40141A	**DKYH4A**	C.	2800	20-23	2150	18-21	500	1-3	200
40145A	**DKX1A**	A/C.	2800	16-18	1400	10-12	525	3-6	200
40154A	**DVXH4A**	C.	2800	18-20	1500	7-10	900	1-3	600
40160B	**D3A6**	C.	1500	16-18	600	8-11	300	1-4	100
40186A	**D3A4**	C.	1700	23-27	750	13.5-16.5	300	1-5	150
40229A	**D3A4**	C.	1700	16-18	800	8.5-11	350	0.5-3.5	175
40230A	**DVXH4A**	C.	3100	20-22	1600	11-13	900	1-3	600
40237A	**DKYH4A**	C.	2500	9-11	1150	6-8	350	1-4	200

40243A	**D3A4**	C.	2000	14-16	450	4.5-6.5	275	0.5-3.5	150
40244A	**DM2P4**	C.	3000	6-8	1500	3-5	1057	0.5-2.5	600
40251A	**DKYH4A**	C.	2700	9-11	1000	4.5-6.5	450	0.5-2.5	175
40266A	**DVZ6A**	C.	2200	11.5-13.5	1100	5-7.5	700	1-3.5	300
40271A	**DKYH4A**	C.	2700	9-11	1000	4.5-6.5	450	0.5-2.5	175
40284A	**DM2P4**	C.	1200	9-11	800	6.5-8.5	600	5.5-7	100
40284E	**DM2P4**	C.	2500	14-16	1325	6-8.5	800	1-3	200
40298A	**D3A4**	C.	1700	9-11	450	4.5-6.5	325	2-5	100
40299A	**DM2P4**	C.	3000	17-19	1500	8.5-10.5	550	0.5-2.5	200
40305A	**DM6**	C.	1800	11-13	575	4.5-6.5	350	0.5-2.5	200
40308A	**DM6**	C.	2800	13-15	1350	7-9.5	550	1-3	180
40310A	**DM6**	C.	1800	11-13	575	4.5-6.5	350	0.5-2.5	200
40317A	**DM2P4**	C.	1300	9-11	650	3-6	500	0.5-3.5	250
40320A	**DM2P4**	C.	2500	16-18	1250	8-10	600	1-3	325
40321A	**DM2P4**	C.	2000	18-20	1100	8-11	675	0-3	450
40330A	**DM2P4**	C.	3100	20-22	1250	6-8	750	0-1	600
40334A	**D3A6**	C.	1500	16-18	600	8-11	300	1-4	100
40355A	**DM2A4**	C.	3000	17-19	1500	8.5-10.5	550	0.5-2.5	200
40359A	**DM6**	C.	1500	13-15	600	6-8	270	0-1	200
40364A	**DM6**	C.	1500	13-15	600	6-8	270	0-1	200
40371A	**DM6**	C.	2800	13-15	1350	7-9.5	550	1-3	180
40373A	**D3A6**	C.	1500	16-18	600	8-11	300	1-4	100
40374A	**D3A4**	C.	1700	21-23	450	8-12	200	0-3	100
40382A	**D3AH4**	A/C.	1000	20-23	500	9-13	325	1-5	200
40402A	**D2A4**	C.	2500	6-8	1100	2-4	700	0-2	300
40403A	**DM2P4**	C.	2700	13-15	600	6.5-9	200	0-2	75
40404A	**DM6**	C.	11.5-13.5		1100	5-7.5	700	1-3.5	300

Service No.	Model	Rotation	Run up to (Rev/Min)	Advance to be (Degrees)	Intermediate Advance I (Rev/Min)	I (Degrees)	II (Rev/Min)	II (Degrees)	No advance Below (Rev/Min)
40410A	**DMBZ4**	C.	2800	19-21	1200	7-9	525	0-2	325
40416A	**D2AH4**	C.	3500	18-21	1500	7-9.5	500	0-2	300
40423A	**DM6**	C.	2000	14.5-16.5	600	6-8	300	0-1	200
40424A	**DM6**	C.	2000	14.5-16.5	600	6-8	300	0-1	200
40427A	**DM2P4**	C.	3000	18-20	1100	11-13	350	0.5-2.5	200
40427D	**DM2P4**	C.	2800	16-18	1250	7-9	600	0.5-2.5	350
40428A	**DM2P4**	C.	2500	16-18	1100	8-10	475	103	220
40438A	**DM2P4**	C.	2000	9-11	1250	7-9	450	0.5-2.5	150
40442A	**DM6**	C.	1500	11-13	530	7-9	300	0-5	150
40459A	**DMBZ6A**	C.	2500	12.5-14.5	1100	8-10	450	0.5-2.5	230
40462A	**DX6A**	C.	3000	15-17	650	7.5-9.5	325	1-5	200
40467A	**DM6**	A.	2000	9-11	925	5-7	700	3-5	250
40469A	**DM2P4**	C.	2500	16-18	1100	8-10	475	1-3	220
40472A	**DM6**	C.	2500	20-23	1650	18-20	350	0.5-3	150
40474A	**DU8A**	A/C.	2500	14-15.5	1100	9-11	375	0.5-3	200
40480A	**DM2P4**	C.	2700	13-15	750	8.5-10.5	200	0-2	100
40483A	**DU8A**	A/C.	2500	14-15.5	1400	11-12.5	475	3-5.5	250
40490A	**DM2P4**	C.	3000	16-18	1300	9-11	500	3-6	250
40492A	**DM2P4**	C.	2500	16-18	1100	8-10	475	1-3	220
40494A	**DM2P4**	C.	3000	17-19	1500	8.5-10.5	375	0-1	200
40495A	**DM2P4**	C.	2500	16-18	1250	8-10	600	1-3	325
40496A	**DM2P4**	C.	2000	18-20	1100	8-11	675	0-3	450

40497A	**DM2P4**	C.	2500	14-16	1325	6-8.5	800	1-3	200
40499A	**DM2P4**	C.	2800	16-18	1250	7-9	600	0.5-2.5	350
40502A	**DM2A4**	C.	3000	17-19	1500	8.5-10.5	550	0.5-2	200
40504A	**DM2P4**	C.	3100	20-22	1250	6-8	750	0-1	600
40510A	**DM2P4**	C.	1500	11-13	650	6-8	300	0.5-2.5	150
40512A	**DM2P4**	C.	3000	6-8	1500	3-5	1075	0.5-2.5	600
40528A	**DMBZ6**	C.	3200	20-23	1100	11-13	450	0.5-3.5	300
40530A	**DM2P4**	C.	3000	16-18	1300	9-11	500	3-6	250
40532A	**DM6**	C.	1500	11-13	500	7-9	300	1.5-4.5	150
40535A	**DM2P4**	C.	2000	9-11	1250	7-9	450	0.5-2.5	150
40543A	**DM2P4**	C.	2600	10-12	1000	7-9	400	0.5-2.5	225
40545A	**DM6**	C.	2800	13-15	1200	9-11	600	1.5-3.5	325
40546A	**DM6**	C.	2600	10-12	1000	7.5-9.5	500	1-3	350
40548A	**DM2P4**	C.	1300	9-11	650	3-6	350	0-1	250
40548B	**CM2P4**	C.	3000	10-12	900	4.5-6.5	500	0.5-3	275
40549A	**D3A4**	C.	2000	11-13	1450	10-13	1100	1.5-5.5	875
40549B	**D3A4**	C.	2000	18-20	950	14-16	430	6-10	200
40551A	**DXH6A**	A/C.	3000	14-16	550	6-8	350	1-4	200
40552A	**DM2P4**	C.	2500	16-18	1100	8-10	475	1-3	220
40556A	**DUH6A**	C.	2500	20-23	1050	10-12	350	0.5-3	150
40557A	**DMBZ6**	C.	3500	24-26	1400	15-17	500	1-3	300
40559A	**DM2P4**	C.	2800	7-9	1100	2.5-4.5	250	0-1	100
40560A	**DM2P4**	A/C.	2000	16018	500	5-7	250	0-1.5	200
40561A	**DM2P4**	C.	2800	15-17	900	6-8	500	1-3.5	200
40561B	**DM2P4**	C.	2800	12-14	1000	5-7	600	0-2	450
40566A	**D3A4**	C.	1800	18-20	850	14-16	450	2-5	300
40569A	**DM2P4**	C.	2800	16-18	1300	8-10.5	750	1-3.5	450

Service No.	Model	Rotation	Run up to (Rev/ Min)	Advance to be (Degrees)	Intermediate Advance I (Rev/ Min)	Intermediate Advance I (Degrees)	Intermediate Advance II (Rev/ Min)	Intermediate Advance II (Degrees)	No advance Below (Rev/ Min)
40570A	**DM2P4**	C.	2400	11-13	1130	6-8	450	0.5-2.5	150
40571A	**DM2P4**	C.	1300	9-11	650	3-6	500	0.5-3.5	250
40572A	**DM6**	C.	2000	9-11	650	4-6	400	0.5-2.5	225
40573A	**18D2**	A/C.	2000	14-16	1000	8-13	500	1-5	200
40574A	**DM2P4**	C.	2000	16-18	1350	14-16	700	3-5	200
40574B	**DM2P4**	C.	1500	9-11	900	5.5-8	650	0-2.5	525
40576A	**DMBZ6**	C.	3200	17-19	1000	10-12	450	0.5-3.5	275
40577A	**DMBZ6**	C.	1500	8-10	1130	6-8	450	0.5-2.5	150
40577B	**DMBZ6**	C.	2000	7-9	1000	5-7	450	0.5-2.5	150
40578A	**DMBZ6**	C.	3500	16-18	1300	10-12	650	0.5-3.5	400
40579A	**D2AH4**	C.	2800	16-18	1250	7-9	600	0.5-2.5	350
40580A	**DM6**	C.	2000	14-16	500	3-6	400	0-3	300
40581A	**DM6**	C.	2000	14-16	500	3-6	400	0-3	300
40582A	**D3AH4**	C.	2800	12-14	1950	10-12	850	3-5	450
40583A	**DM2P4**	C.	2200	12-14	850	1-3	650	0-1	500
40586A	**D2A4**	A/C.	2000	7-9	1000	3-4.5	600	0.5-2	300
40587A	**DM2P4**	C.	2000	13-15	600	4.5-6.5	400	0-2.5	300
40589A	**18D2**	A/C.	1600	11-13	1000	6-10	750	0-4.5	550
40594A	**DM2P4**	C.	2600	10-12	1000	3-5	500	0-2	150
40597A	**DM2P4**	C.	1500	11-13	550	5.5-7.5	325	0.5-2.5	200
40598A	**DM2P4**	C.	3000	15-17	1650	11-13	650	4-7	350
40600A	**DM2P4**	C.	2400	11-13	1130	6-8	450	0.5-2.5	150

40601A	**DM6**	C.	1500	11-13	800	8-11	370	0-3	200
40602A	**DMX6A**	C.	3000	20-23	1450	13-15	500	6-9	225
40603A	**DM2P4**	C.	3000	12-14	1450	6-8	550	0.5-2.5	150
40603E	**DM2P4**	C.	3000	14 max.	1450	6-8	600	0.5-2.5	250
40604A	**DM2P4**	C.	3000	11-13	1200	4-6	300	0-1	100
40604E	**DM2P4**	C.	3000	13 max.	1200	4-6	350	0-1	200
40605A	**DM2P4**	C.	2600	19-21	1100	11.5-13.5	350	3.5-6.5	150
40606A	**DM2P4**	C.	3000	15-17	1650	11-13	650	4-7	350
40607A	**DM2P4**	C.	3200	18-20	450	6-10	325	1-5	225
40608A	**DMBX6**	C.	2500	16-18	900	9.5-11.5	300	1-3	100
40609A	**DM2P4**	C.	2800	19 max.	600	9-11	300	1.5-4.5	150
40609B	**DM2P4**	C.	2700	19-21	600	6-8	400	2.5-5.5	130
40610A	**18D2**	C.	1600	11-13	1000	6-10	750	0-4.5	550
40611A	**DM2P4**	C.	3500	16-18	1000	9.5-11.5	450	1-3	270
40611B	**DM2P4**	C.	3000	14-17	1100	7.5-9.5	600	0-3	400
40612A	**DM6**	A/C.	2400	11-13	1100	5.5-7.5	700	2-4.5	130
40613A	**DMBZ6A**	C.	2000	7-9	1000	5-7	450	0.5-2.5	150
40614A	**DM6**	C.	2500	13-15.5	800	9.5-12	400	0-3	275
40616A	**DMBZ6**	C.	2000	8-10	1150	4-6	700	0-2	500
40617A	**DMBZ6**	C.	2000	10-12	850	7-9	450	0-2.5	325
40618A	**DVX6A**	C.	3200	20-23	1100	11-13	450	0.5-3.5	300
40619A	**DVX6A**	C.	3200	17-19	1000	10-12	450	0.5-3.5	275
40620A	**DM2P4**	C.	3000	20-23	1350	11-13	600	4.5-6.5	300
40622A	**DM2P4**	C.	3000	20-23	1350	11-13	600	4.5-6.5	300
40623A	**DM2P4**	C.	3000	14-17	1100	7.5-9.5	600	0-3	400
40624A	**DM2P4**	C.	2800	16-18	1250	7-9	600	0.5-2.5	350
40625A	**DM2P4**	C.	2000	16-18	850	5-7	450	0.5-2.5	200

Service No.	Model	Rotation	Run up to (Rev/ Min)	Advance to be (Degrees)	(Rev/ Min)	Intermediate Advance I (Degrees)	(Rev/ Min)	II (Degrees)	No advance Below (Rev/ Min)
40626A	**DM2P4**	C.	2300	15.5 max.	1500	11-13	550	1-3	275
40629A	**DX6A**	A/C.	1800	15-17	950	12-14	350	0.5-3.5	200
40631A	**DM2P4**	C.	2600	10-12	1000	7-9	400	0.5-2.5	225
40632A	**DM2P4**	C.	2600	12-14	1300	9-11	550	0.5-2.5	225
40633A	**DM6**	C.	2600	10-12	1000	7.5-9.5	700	5-7	350
40634A	**DM6**	C.	2800	13-15	1200	9-11	600	1.5-3.5	325
40635A	**DM6**	C.	1500	11-13	500	7-9	300	1.5-4.5	150
40636A	**DM2P4**	C.	3000	13 max.	1200	4-6	350	0-1	200
40637A	**DM2P4**	C.	3000	17 max.	1650	11-13	650	4-7	350
40638A	**DM2P4**	C.	3000	14-17	1100	7.5-9.5	600	0-3	400
40639A	**DM2P4**	C.	3200	18-20	450	6-10	325	1-5	225
40640A	**DMBZ6**	C.	3400	19 max.	1300	10-12	500	1-3	250
40641A	**DMBZ6**	A/C.	3000	11-13	1500	8.5-10.5	900	5.5-7.5	150
40643A	**DM2P4**	C.	2400	11-13	1500	9-11	450	0.5-2.5	150
40644A	**DM2P4**	C.	2000	13-15	1225	11-13	500	2.5-5.5	300
40646A	**18D2**	A/C.	2800	13-15	1300	7-9	600	1-3	250
40647A	**DM2P4**	C.	2300	17 max.	1500	11-13	900	1-4	350
40648A	**DM2P4**	C.	2200	17 max.	650	8-10	350	1.5-3.5	250
40648B	**DM2P4**	C.	2200	17 max.	650	8-10	350	0.5-3.5	250
40649A	**DM2P4**	A/C.	3000	18-20	2000	15-17	600	5-8	250
40649B	**DM2P4**	A/C.	3000	17-19	1800	11-13	550	0.5-2.5	250
40650A	**DMBZ6**	C.	2000	15 max.	1200	10.5-12.5	400	1.5-4.5	250

40650B	**DMBZ6**	C.	2000	13-15	1400	12-14	550	2.5-4.5	225
40651A	**DM2P4**	C.	2600	14.5-16.5	850	4-6	400	0-2	150
40652A	**DM2P4**	C.	2800	12-14	1750	9-11	800	4-6	250
40653A	**DM2P4**	C.	2300	17 max.	1500	11-13	700	0-2	350
40653E	**DM2P4**	C.	2500	14 max.	1100	5.5-7.5	600	0-2	250
40655A	**23D4**	C.	2500	6-8	1100	2-4	700	0-2	300
40656A	**DM2P4**	C.	1800	15 max.	950	9.5-11.5	550	0.5-3.5	400
40657A	**DMZ6**	A/C.	1600	8-10	850	6-8	450	1-3	225
40658A	**DM2P4**	C.	3000	20-23	1350	11-13	500	2-5	300
40659A	**D3AH4**	C.	2500	9-11	1050	4.5-6.5	400	0-2	250
40660A	**DM6**	C.	1200	9-11	600	5-7	350	0-2	225
40661A	**DM6**	C.	2000	14-16	1150	12-14	500	3-6	300
40662A	**DM6**	C.	2000	14-16	1150	12-14	500	3-6	300
40663A	**D3A6**	C.	1500	18-20	600	8-11	300	1-4	150
40665A	**DMBZ6**	C.	2000	13 max.	1100	8-10	550	2.5-4.5	225
40666A	**DUH6A**	A/C.	1200/1470	11 max.	550/700	5	300/450	1	150
40667A	**DM2P4**	A/C.	1800	23 max.	1050	17-19	450	5-8	200
40668A	**DVZ6A**	C.	1600	11-13	950	9-11	350	1-3	150
40670A	**DMBZ6**	C.	1500	11 max.	950	9-11	800	6.5-8.5	230
40671A	**DMBZ6A**	C.	1500	14 max.	1000	12-14	800	8.5-10.5	200
40672A	**DM2P4**	C.	2000	18-20	1100	8-11	675	0-3	500
40673A	**DM6**	C.	2500	20-23	1050	10-12	350	0.5-3	150
40674A	**DM2P4**	C.	2500	16-18.5	1200	6.5-9	750	1-3.5	450
40675A	**DM2P4**	C.	2800	12-14	1500	7.5-9.5	850	3-5	300
40676A	**20D8**	C.	2500	10.5-12.5	900	7-9	400	0.5-3	230
40677A	**D3AH4**	C.	1500	15 max.	800	8-11	475	0-3	350
40678A	**D2A4**	A/C.	800	11 max.	550	9-11	300	0-3	200

Service No.	Model	Rotation	Run up to (Rev/Min)	Advance to be (Degrees)	Intermediate Advance (Rev/Min) I	(Degrees)	(Rev/Min) II	(Degrees)	No advance Below (Rev/Min)
40679A	**DZS4**	C.	2700	21 max.	1750	15-17	400	2.5-5.5	130
40679B	**DZS4**	C.	2700	21 max.	1750	15-17	450	2-6	225
40680A	**DZS4A**	C.	2700	21 max.	1750	15-17	400	2.5-5.5	130
40680B	**DZS4A**	C.	2700	21 max.	1750	15-17	450	2-6	225
40681A	**DM2P4**	C.	3000	16-18	2100	14-16	650	5-7	250
40682A	**DM2P4**	C.	2500	16-18	1100	8-10	475	1-3	220
40683A	**DM2P4**	C.	2000	9-11	1375	8.5-10.5	500	1-3	250
40684A	**DMZ6A**	C.	1600	11-13	950	9-11	350	1-3	150
40685A	**DM6**	C.	1500	9 max.	700	3-5	500	0.5-2.5	325
40686A	**21D6**	C.	2400	14-16	1450	11.5-13.5	900	6.5-9.5	500
40687A	**DM2P4**	C.	3000	16-18	2100	14-16	650	5-7	250
40688A	**DM2P4**	C.	2500	16-18	1625	14-16	475	1-3	220
40689A	**D2A4**	C.	3000	16-18	2100	14-16	650	5-7	250
40690A	**18D2**	A/C.	2000	11-13	1000	8.5-11.5	750	4.5-7.5	300
40691A	**DM2P4**	C.	2800	12-14	2450	12-14	800	4-6	250
40692A	**DM2P4**	C.	3500	14 max.	1800	9-11	700	6.5-9.5	250
40793A	**DMBZ6**	C.	2800	18-20	1525	12.5-14.5	925	6.5-8.5	350
40694A	**DMBZ6**	C.	3200	13-15	2150	11-13	800	5-7	160
40695A	**DMBZ6**	C.	2000	13-15	1050	6-8	650	1-3	400
40696A	**DMBZ6**	C.	2500	13-15	1200	7-9	300	0-1.5	175
40697A	**DMBZ6A**	C.	1500	14 max.	800	8.5-10.5	400	1.5-3.5	200
40698A	**DM2P4**	C.	2700	13-15	750	8.5-10.5	350	0-3	225

40703A	**18D2**	A/C.	1200	9-11	600	5-7	350	0-2	225
40703B	**18D2**	A/C.	1750	9-11	1100	7.5-10.5	650	1-4	375
40704A	**24D6**	A/C.	2400	11-13	1100	5.5-7.5	700	2.5-4.5	130
40705A	**DM2P4**	C.	2500	16-18	1100	8-10	475	1-3	220
40706A	**D2A4**	C.	2500	6-8	1900	6-8	1100	2-4	300
40707A	**DM2P4**	C.	2600	13 max.	1650	7-9	850	0.5-2.5	500
40707D	**DM2P4**	C.	3000	13 max.	1950	7.5-9.5	850	0.5-2.5	425
40708A	**DM2P4**	C.	2800	7-9	1700	5-7	625	0.5-2.5	200
40709A	**DM2P4**	C.	2800	14-16	1550	11-13	450	3-6	250
40710A	**18D2**	A/C.	1750	9-11	1100	7.5-10.5	650	1-4	375
40711A	**23D4**	C.	2500	6-8	1100	2-4	700	0-2	300
40713A	**DM6**	C.	1200	9-11	600	5-7	350	0-2	225
40714A	**DM6**	C.	1500	9 max.	700	3-5	500	0.5-2.5	325
40715A	**20D8**	C.	2500	10.5-12.5	900	7-9	400	0.5-3	230
40716A	**DM6**	C.	2500	15 max.	1300	11.5-13.5	700	6.5-9.5	300
40717A	**23D4**	A/C.	2600	22.5 max.	1550	16.5-18.5	550	6-9	225
40718A	**23D4**	C.	3500	14 max.	1800	9-11	700	6.5-8.5	250
40719A	**DMBZ6**	C.	1500	12 max.	800	5.5-7.5	500	0.5-2.5	300
40720A	**DMBZ6**	C.	2500	12.5-14.5	1400	9.5-11.5	900	6-8	230
40721A	**DMBZ6**	C.	2000	7-9	1000	5-7	450	0.5-2.5	150
40721D	**DMBZ6**	C.	2000	6-7.5	1000	5-7	450	0.5-2.5	150
40722A	**DM2P4**	A/C.	2000	14-16	900	7-10	300	0-1.5	150
40723A	**DM2P4**	A/C.	2000	18 max.	1000	10-12	400	2.5-6	200
40724A	**DM2P4**	A/C.	2200	15-17	1600	14-16	950	6-8	300
40725A	**DM6**	C.	2500	15 max.	1300	11.5-13.5	700	6.5-9.5	300
40726A	**DM2P4**	A/C.	1800	23 max.	1050	17-19	450	5-8	200
40726B	**DM2P4**	A/C.	2000	20-23	800	9-11.5	450	1-4	280

Service No.	Model	Rotation	Run up to (Rev/ Min)	Advance to be (Degrees)	Intermediate Advance I (Rev/ Min)	I (Degrees)	II (Rev/ Min)	II (Degrees)	No advance Below (Rev/ Min)
40727A	**23D4**	C.	FIXED AUTO ADVANCE MECHANISM SPEED LIMITED 2800-3000 DISTRIBUTOR REV/MIN						
40728A	**DM6**	A/C.	3000	11-13	1150	7.5-9.5	350	0-2	150
40729A	**DMBZ6**	C.	3200	14 max.	1800	9.5-11.5	800	5-7	180
40730A	**DM6**	C.	1800	12 max.	850	7-9	400	0-2	275
40731A	**23D4**	C.	2000	9-11	1375	8.5-10.5	500	1-3	150
40732A	**DW13A8**	A/C.	2500	14-15.5	1400	11-12.5	540	4.75-6.25	150
40733A	**DM6**	C.	2800	13-15	1350	7-9.5	550	1-3	180
40734A	**DM2P4**	C.	2800	14-16	1550	11-13	450	3-6	250
40735A	**DM2P4**	C.	1200	9-11	600	5-7	350	0-2	225
40736A	**DM2P4**	C.	2200	12-14	1500	9.5-11.5	650	0-1	500
40737A	**DU8A**	A/C.	2000	9-11	810	4.5-6.5	300	0-1.25	180
40738A	**DZS4A**	C.	3100	20-22	1600	11-13	750	0-1	625
40739A	**DM6**	C.	1500	11-13	800	8-11	370	0-3	200
40740A	**DMBZ6A**	C.	1500	14 max.	800	8.5-10.5	400	1.5-3.5	200
40741A	**DM6**	C.	1500	13-15	600	6-8	270	0-1	200
40742A	**DM6**	C.	2400	14-16	1800	13.5-15.5	450	1-3	125
40743A	**DM2P4**	C.	2500	10 max.	1250	5-7	450	0.5-2.5	120
40744A	**DM2P4**	C.	3000	12.5-14.5	1500	8-10	700	0.5-3	575
40745A	**DM2P4**	C.	3000	14.5-16.5	2050	11.5-13.5	800	0.5-2.5	575
40746A	**DMBZ6**	C.	3200	14 max.	1800	9.5-11.5	800	5-7	180
40747A	**25D6**	C.	1500	7-9	900	6-8	400	0.5-2.5	220

40748A	**D3A4**	C.	1500	18 max.	800	11.5-13.5	450	3.5-5.5	250
40749A	**DMB6**	C.	2000	12 max.	850	7-9	450	0-2.5	325
40750A	**DM6**	C.	2600	17 max.	1100	9.5-11.5	450	1-3	250
40752A	**DM2P4**	C.	2200	16 max.	1300	11-13	500	4-6.5	250
40753A	**DZS4A**	C.	2700	21 max.	1750	15-17	600	6-8	225
40754A	**DM2P4**	C.	2500	16 max.	1500	9-11	450	0.5-2.5	150
40755A	**DM2P4**	C.	2000	16 max.	1050	7-9	600	1-3	370
40757A	**23D4**	C.	1500	15 max.	600	7-9	350	0.5-2.5	250
40758A	**DM6**	C.	2000	9-11	650	4-6	400	0.5-2.5	225
40759A	**DM2P4**	C.	1500	9-11	900	5.5-8	650	0-2.5	525
40760A	**DM2P4**	C.	1200	9-11	500	1-4	400	0-1.5	300
40761A	**DM2P4**	C.	2500	13-15	750	8-10	400	1-3	250
40762A	**DM2P4**	A/C.	2600	12-14	1500	9-11	450	4.5-7	200
40763A	**DM2P4**	C.	2700	13-15	1350	10.5-12	450	4-7	175
40764A	**DM2P4**	C.	3000	16-18	1300	9-11	500	3-6	250
40765A	**DM2P4**	C.	2500	16-18	1100	8-10	475	1-3	220
40766A	**DM2P4**	C.	2000	9-11	900	4.5-6.5	500	1-3	150
40767A	**25D4**	C.	3000	13 max.	1950	7.5-9.5	850	0.5-2.5	425
40768A	**25D4**	C.	2200	17 max.	1250	12-14	350	0.5-2.5	250
40769A	**25D4**	C.	2500	16-18.5	1200	6.5-9	750	1-3.5	450
40770A	**25D4**	C.	2800	15-17	1100	8-10	500	1-3.5	200
40771A	**25D4**	C.	2500	16-18.5	1200	6.5-9	750	1-3.5	450
40772A	**25D4**	C.	2800	12-14	1500	7.5-9.5	600	0-2	300
40773A	**25D4**	C.	2200	16 max.	700	7.5-9.5	350	0-2.5	250
40774A	**25D4**	C.	1200	9-11	500	1-4	400	0-1.5	300
40775A	**25D4**	C.	2800	16-18	1250	7-9	600	0.5-2.5	250
40776A	**25D4**	C.	2800	16-18	1250	7-9	600	0.5-2.5	250

Service No.	Model	Rotation	Run up to (Rev/Min)	Advance to be (Degrees)	Intermediate Advance I (Rev/Min)	Intermediate Advance I (Degrees)	Intermediate Advance II (Rev/Min)	Intermediate Advance II (Degrees)	No advance Below (Rev/Min)
40777A	**25D4**	C.	2500	16 max.	1500	9-11	450	0.5-2.5	150
40778A	**25D4**	C.	2400	11-13	1130	6-8	450	0.5-2.5	150
40779A	**25D4**	C.	2000	13-15	600	4.5-6.5	400	0-2.5	300
40780A	**25D4**	C.	1500	11-13	650	6-8	300	0.5-2.5	150
40781A	**25D4**	C.	2800	14-16	1400	3.5-6.5	1000	0-3	550
40781B	**25D4**	C.	2000	13-15	1225	11-13	500	2.5-5.5	300
40782A	**25D4**	C.	2400	11-13	1130	6-8	450	0.5-2.5	150
40783A	**25D4**	C.	2500	13-15	750	8-10	400	1-3	250
40784A	**25D4**	C.	2200	12-14	1200	5.5-7.5	650	0-1	500
40785A	**25D4**	C.	2000	18-20	1100	8-11	675	0-3	500
40786A	**25D4**	C.	3000	17-19	1500	8.5-10.5	550	0.5-2.5	250
40787A	**25D4**	C.	3000	20-23	1350	11-13	500	2-5	250
40788A	**25D4**	C.	3000	17 max.	1650	11-13	500	0.5-3.5	350
40789A	**25D4**	C.	3000	14-17	1100	7.5-9.5	600	0-3	400
40790A	**25D4**	C.	2000	16 max.	1050	7-9	600	1-3	370
40791A	**25D4**	C.	2500	10 max.	1250	5-7	450	0.5-2.5	120
40792A	**25D4**	C.	2800	14-16	1550	11-13	450	3-6	250
40793A	**25D4**	C.	2800	7-9	1100	2.5-4.5	400	0-1	200
40794A	**25D4**	C.	2800	14-16	1550	11-13	450	3-6	250
40795A	**25D4**	C.	1200	9-11	600	5-7	350	0-2	225
40796A	**25D4**	C.	2700	21 max.	1250	11-13	450	2-6	225
40797A	**25D4**	C.	2500	16-18	1100	8-10	475	1-3	220

40798A	**25D4**	C.	3000	16-18	1300	9-11	500	3-6	250
40799A	**25D4**	C.	2000	9-11	900	4.5-6.5	500	1-3	150
40800A	**25D4**	A/C.	2000	18 max.	1000	10-12	400	2.5-6	200
40801A	**25D4**	A/C.	2200	15-17	950	6-8	475	0-2	300
40802A	**25D4**	A/C.	2000	20-23	800	9-11.5	450	1-4	280
40803A	**25D4**	C.	3000	14.5-16.5	1050	11.5-13.5	1100	3.5-5.5	575
40804A	**25D4**	C.	3000	12.5-14.5	1500	8-10	700	0.5-3	575
40805A	**25D4**	C.	3000	14.5-16.5	2050	11.5-13.5	1100	3.5-5.5	575
40806A	**25D4**	C.	3000	12.5-14.5	1500	8-10	700	0.5-3	575
40807A	**25D4**	C.	2600	12-14	1300	9-11	550	0.5-2.5	325
40808A	**25D4**	C.	2600	10-12	1000	7-9	400	0.5-2.5	225
40809A	**25D4**	C.	1500	9-11	900	5.5-8	650	0-2.5	525
40810A	**25D4**	C.	1500	9-11	900	5.5-8	650	0-2.5	525
40811A	**25D4**	C.	2600	12-14	1300	9-11	550	0.5-2.5	325
40812A	**25D4**	C.	1600	10-12	1000	7-9	400	0.5-2.5	225
40813A	**25D4**	C.	1500	12-14	550	5.5-7.5	325	0.5-2.5	200
40814A	**DM2**	C.	3000	14.5-16.5	1500	8-10	800	0.5-2.5	575
40815A	**DM2**	C.	3000	14.5-16.5	1500	8-10	800	0.5-2.5	575
40816A	**25D6**	C.	2000	14-16	650	6.5-8.5	400	0-3	300
40817A	**DM2**	C.	2700	21 max.	1250	11-13	450	2-6	225
40818A	**DM2**	C.	2400	11-13	1130	6-8	450	0.5-2.5	150
40819A	**23D4**	C.	3800	14-16	800	5-7	300	0-1.5	225
40820A	**18D2**	A/C.	1750	4-6	600	0-3	200	0-1.5	375
40821A	**25D4**	C.	2500	16 max.	1500	9-11	450	0.5-2.5	150
40822A	**25D4**	C.	2000	11.5-13.5	700	5-7	400	0-1.5	325
40822B	**25D4**	C.	2300	12-14	700	4-6	400	0-2	300
40823A	**25D4**	C.	2300	12-14	1350	8.5-10.5	400	0-2	300

Service No.	Model	Rotation	Run up to (Rev/ Min)	Advance to be (Degrees)	Intermediate Advance (Rev/ Min) I	(Degrees)	(Rev/ Min) II	(Degrees)	No advance Below (Rev/ Min)
40824A	**25D6**	C.	1200	9-11	600	5-7	350	0-2	225
40825A	**25D6**	C.	1500	9 max.	700	3-5	500	0.5-2.5	325
40826A	**25D6**	C.	1500	13-15	600	6-8	400	1.5-4	225
40827A	**25D6**	C.	2400	14-16	1100	7.5-9.5	450	1-3	175
40828A	**DMBZ6**	C.	2300	8.5-10.5	800	5-7	650	2-4	400
40829A	**23D4**	A/C.	800	11 max.	450	5.5-8.5	300	0-3	200
40830A	**25D6**	C.	2500	16 max.	600	5-7	250	0-1	200
40831A	**DM2**	C.	2300	14.5 max.	500	6-8.5	300	0-3	200
40832A	**DMBZ6**	C.	2000	7-9	1000	5-7	450	0.5-2.5	150
40833A	**25D6**	C.	1800	12 max.	850	7-9	400	0-2	275
40834A	**25D6**	C.	2600	17 max.	1100	9.5-11.5	450	1-3	250
40835A	**25D4**	C.	2000	16 max.	1050	7-9	600	1-3	370
40836A	**DM2**	C.	2700	13-15	450	4-7	300	0-3	175
40837A	**25D4**	C.	2700	13-15	450	4-7	300	0-3	175
40838A	**DM6**	C.	1500	13-15	600	6-8	400	1.5-4	225
40839A	**DM6**	C.	2400	14-16	1100	7.5-9.5	450	1-3	175
40840A	**25D6**	C.	3000	12 max.	950	5.5-7.5	600	1-3	375
40841A	**25D6**	C.	3000	10 max.	900	5.5-7.5	400	1-3	325
40842A	**25D4**	C.	2500	9 max.	1350	4-6	700	0.5-2.5	250
40843A	**18D2**	C.	1500	6-8	750	5-7	500	1-3	300
40845A	**25D6**	C.	2000	9-11	650	4-6	400	0.5-2.5	225
40847A	**25D4**	C.	1800	13 max.	1000	8-10	450	1.5-3.5	180

40848A	**DMBZ6**	C.	2500	11.5-13.5	1000	7-9	450	0.5-2.5	250
40848B	**DMBZ6**	C.	2500	11.5-13.5	1000	7-9	450	0.5-2.5	200
40849A	**25D4**	C.	3200	17 max.	1850	12-14	450	0.5-2.5	250
40849B	**25D4**	C.	3200	15-17	1250	8-10	400	0.5-2.5	100
40850A	**25D4**	C.	1200	5-7	600	2-4	500	0.5-2.5	300
40851A	**25D4**	C.	2500	13.5	1250	8-10	650	1-3	400
40852A	**25D4**	C.	2800	11 max.	1000	5-7	600	0-2	400
40853A	**25D4**	C.	3200	17 max.	1850	12-14	450	0.5-2.5	250
40853B	**25D4**	C.	2500	14-16	850	6.5-8.5	500	1.5-5.5	250
40854A	**25D4**	C.	3000	14.5-16.5	1500	8-10	800	0.5-2.5	575
40854B	**25D4**	C.	2800	13.5-15.5	1600	9.5-11.75	800	1.5-2.5	575
40855A	**25D4**	C.	3000	12.5-14.5	1500	8-10	700	0.5-3	575
40855B	**25D4**	C.	2800	13.5-15.75	1600	9.5-11.5	700	1-3	550
40856A	**25D4**	C.	3000	14.5-16.5	1500	8-10	800	0.5-2.5	575
40856D	**25D4**	C.	2800	13.5-15.5	1600	9.5-11.5	800	0.5-2.5	575
40857A	**25D4**	C.	3000	12.5-14.5	1500	8-10	700	0.5-3	575
40857D	**25D4**	C.	2800	13.5-15.5	1600	9.5-11.5	700	1-3	550
40858A	**DM2**	C.	2600	10-12	1000	7-9	400	0.5-2.5	225
40859A	**DM2**	C.	2500	16-18	1100	8-10	475	1-3	220
40860A	**DM2**	C.	3000	16-18	1300	9-11	400	0.5-3.5	250
40861A	**23D4**	C.	2800	12-14	1500	7.5-9.5	600	0-2	300
40862A	**23D4**	C.	2000	12-15	1100	7-10.5	400	0-2	200
40863A	**DMBZ6**	C.	2500	10-12	1300	7-9	450	0.5-2.5	125
40864A	**DMBZ6**	C.	3300	11-13	1750	7-9	500	2-4	100
40865A	**25D6**	C.	2700	13-15	1200	9-11	500	1-3	200
40866A	**25D6**	C.	2000	14-16	1150	12-14	500	3-6	300
40866E	**25D6**	C.	2000	12014	650	6.5-8.5	400	0-3	300

Service No.	Model	Rotation	Run up to (Rev/Min)	Advance to be (Degrees)	Intermediate Advance (Rev/Min) I	(Degrees)	(Rev/Min) II	(Degrees)	No advance Below (Rev/Min)
40869A	**25D4**	C.	2700	13-15	1250	10-12	550	5-8	225
40870	**25D4**	A/C.	1500	11-13	750	6.5-8.5	450	1-3	275
40871A	**DMBZ6**	C.	2500	11-13	1100	6.5-8.5	550	1-3	200
40872A	**25D4**	A/C.	1500	11-13	750	6.5-8.5	450	1-3	200
40873A	**25D4**	C.	1800	13-15	1000	10.5-12.5	450	4-6	150
40875A	**25D4**	C.	2700	13-15	1350	10.5-12.5	450	4-7	175
40876A	**DU8A**	A/C.	2500	14-15.5	1100	8.75-10.25	475	3-5.75	250
40877A	**DM2**	C.	2200	17 max.	650	8-10	350	0.5-3.5	250
40878A	**25D6**	C.	1500	11-13	800	8-11	370	0-3	200
40879A	**DMBZ6**	C.	1500	14 max.	800	8.5-10.5	400	1.5-3.5	200
40880A	**23D4**	C.	2500	9-11	1050	4.5-6.5	400	0-2	150
40881A	**23D4**	A/C.	2000	14-16	950	11-13	500	0.5-4.5	325
40882A	**25D6**	C.	2600	11-13	800	6-8	400	2.5-4.5	200
40883A	**22D6**	C.	3500	24-26	1400	15-17	500	1-3	300
40883B	**22D6**	C.	3500	24-26	1400	15-17	500	1-3	200
40884A	**22D6**	C.	3200	20-23	1700	14-16	600	3.5-6.5	300
40884B	**22D6**	C.	3200	20-23	1700	14-16	600	3.5-6.5	200
40885A	**22D6**	C.	3400	19 max.	1300	10-12	500	1-3	250
40885B	**22D6**	C.	3400	19 max.	1300	10-12	500	1-3	200
40886A	**22D6**	C.	2000	13 max.	800	6-8	400	0.5-2.5	225
40887A	**22D6**	C.	2000	12 max.	850	7-9	450	0-2.5	325
40887B	**22D6**	C.	2000	12 max.	850	7-9	450	0-2.5	250

40888A	**22D6**	C.	2300	8.5-10.5	800	5-7	650	2-4	400
40888B	**22D6**	C.	2300	8.5-10.5	800	5-7	525	0-1.5	300
40889A	**20D8**	C.	2500	10.5-12.5	900	7-9	400	0.5-3	230
40890A	**25D4**	C.	2200	12-14	1200	5.5-7.5	850	1-3	500
40891A	**25D6**	C.	1500	11-13	650	6-8	300	0.5-2.5	150
40892A	**25D4**	C.	2500	16-18	1100	8-10	475	1-3	220
40893A	**25D4**	C.	2000	13-15	1100	8-10	400	0.5-2.5	180
40894A	**25D6**	C.	2000	9-11	950	6-8	400	0.5-2.5	150
40895A	**25D6**	C.	2500	11-13	1400	8-10	400	0-2	200
40895D	**25D6**	C.	2500	11-13	1150	7-9	600	1-3	350
40896A	**25D6**	C.	1500	15-17	1000	11.5-13.5	350	0.5-2.5	200
40896D	**25D6**	C.	2500	15-17	1000	11.5-13.5	450	0-1	350
40897A	**25D4**	C.	1500	9-11	450	3.5-5.5	300	0-3	200
40898A	**20D8**	C.	2000	17-19	750	9.5-11.5	350	1-3	200
40899A	**25D4**	C.	2800	16-18	1250	7-9	600	0.5-2.5	250
40900A	**25D6**	C.	1200	9-11	600	5-7	350	0-2	225
40901A	**25D6**	C.	1800	14-16	750	6-8	400	0.5-2.5	230
40902A	**22D4**	C.	2000	10-12	1000	6.5-8.5	550	0-2	400
40902B	**22D4**	C.	2500	11-13	1000	7-9	400	0-2	300
40903A	**25D4**	C.	1800	9-11	1000	5.5-7.5	500	1-3	180
40904A	**25D6**	C.	1500	11-13	800	8-11	370	0-3	200
40905A	**25D4**	C.	3300	12-14	1000	4-6	400	0-2	100
40906A	**20D8**	C.	2000	19-21	1350	15-17	400	1.5-3.5	250
40907A	**18D2**	A/C.	2000	16-19	1000	8-13	500	1-5	200
40908A	**25D4**	C.	2200	13-15	1400	10-12	600	1.5-4	400
40909A	**DM2P4**	C.	2800	12-14	1500	7.5-9.5	850	3-5	300
40910A	**25D6**	C.	2500	17-19	1750	14-16	500	4-6	200

40911A	**DBCH6A**	C.	2800	13-15	1200	9-11	600	1.5-3.5	325
40913A	**25D4**	C.	2800	16-18	1250	7-9	600	0.5-2.5	250
40914A	**25D4**	C.	3000	20-23	1350	11-13	400	0-2.5	250
40915A	**25D4**	C.	3000	17-19	1500	8.5-10.5	550	0.5-2.5	250
40916A	**25D4**	C.	2500	11-3	500	3.5-5.5	300	0-3	200
40917A	**DMBZ6**	C.	2500	10-12	1300	7-9	450	0.5-2.5	125
40919A	**25D4**	C.	2750	15-17	900	7-9	400	0-0.5	330
40920A	**25D6**	C.	2000	14-16	650	6.5-8.5	400	0-3	300
40921A	**25D6**	C.	2800	13-15	1350	7-9.5	550	1-3	180
40922A	**25D6**	C.	2500	20-23	1050	10-12	350	0.5-3	150
40923A	**25D6**	C.	2500	15-17	1000	11.5-13.5	350	0.5-2.5	200
40924A	**25D4**	C.	2000	9-11	900	4.5-6.5	500	1-3	150

The following Data Tables include Vacuum Codes

The letters "y" and "z" denote types of vacuum connection. Letter "z" is screw type, letter "y" push on.

Service No.	Model	Rotation	Vacuum Code	Run up to (Rev/Min)	Advance to be (Degrees)	Intermediate Advance I (Rev/Min)	(Degrees)	Intermediate Advance II (Rev/Min)	(Degrees)	No advance Below (Rev/Min)
40925A	**23D4**	C.	—	2000	14-16	1000	11-13	300	1-4	125
40926A	**23D4**	C.	—	1700	16-18	800	8.5-11.5	350	0.5-3.5	175
40927A	**25D4**	C.	6/17/7	3200	10.5-12.5	1050	8-10	650	0.5-2.5	525
40927B	**25D4**	C.	6/17/7	3200	12-14	1050	8-10	650	0.5-2.5	525
40928A	**25D6**	C.	4/15/7	2000	11-13	650	6.5-8.5	350	1-3	200
40929A	**DZS4A**	C.	—	2700	21 max.	1250	11-13	450	2-6	225
40930A	**25D4**	C.	1/6/10	3300	12-14	2200	9.5-11.5	350	1.5-5	150
40931A	**25D4**	C.	5/11/7	2800	11-13	1700	8-10	450	0-2	300
40932A	**25D6**	C.	7/15/10	2800	13-15	1350	7-9.5	550	1-3	180
40933A	**25D4**	C.	3/11/12	2200	13-15	1400	10-12	600	1.5-4	400
40934A	**25D4**	C.	5/14/11	3000	16-18	1300	9-11	400	0.5-3.5	250
40935A	**25D4**	C.	5/14/11	2500	16-18	1100	8-10	475	1-3	220
40936A	**DZS4A**	C.	—	2700	21 max.	1250	11-13	450	2-6	225
40937A	**23D4**	C.	—	2800	12-14	1500	7.5-9.5	850	3-5	300
40938A	**DMBZ6**	C.	—	2800	9-11	1200	4-6	400	1-3	200
40939A	**23D4**	C.	—	3500	18-21	1500	7-9.5	500	0-2	300
40940A	**25D4**	C.	5/9/5	2600	14.5-16.5	850	4-6	400	0-2	175
40941A	**25D4**	C.	—	2500	12-14	700	6-8	400	0.5-2.5	240
40942A	**25D4**	C.	4/8/5	3300	13-15	2400	10-12	950	2-4	250
40943A	**23D4**	C.	—	3500	11-13	1000	7-9	450	0-2	200
40944A	**25D4**	C.	4/18/12	2700	21 max.	1250	11-13	450	2-6	225
*40945A	**29D6**	C.	6/11/9	2000	13.5-15.5	1000	10-12	450	0-3.75	190

* This unit to be checked with both rising and falling speeds, commencing with rising speed.

40946A	**25D4**	C.	3/9/8	2200	12-14	750	8-10	400	1-3	250
40947A	**23D4**	C.	—	2200	11-13	900	5.5-7.5	550	1-3	200
40948A	**25D6**	C.	3/10/10	2800	9-11	1500	6-8	550	0.5-2.5	300
40949A	**25D6**	C.	7/15/10	2800	13-15	1350	7.5-9.5	550	1-3	250
40950A	**25D6**	C.	4/17/6	2000	7-9	1000	5-7	450	0.5-2.5	150
40951A	**23D4**	C.	—	2200	11-13	900	5.5-7.5	550	1-3	200
40952A	**25D6**	C.	6/13/5	2500	16-18	1100	11.5-13.5	300	1-3	100
40953A	**23D4**	C.	—	3500	11-13	1000	7-9	450	0-2	200
40954A	**25D6**	C.	6/12/7	1800	10-12	900	7.5-9.5	350	1-3	200
40955A	**25D4**	C.	3/8/7	3300	15-17	900	6-8	400	0.5-2.5	150
40956A	**25D4**	C.	4/8/5	3300	13-15	2400	10-12	950	2-4	205
40957A	**25D4**	C.	4/8/5	2700	13-15	600	8-10.5	400	0-3	175
40958A	**25D4**	C.	3/7/8	3300	16 max.	900	8-10	500	1.5-4.5	200
40959A	**25D4**	C.	4/7/7	1500	10-12	500	4.5-6.5	250	0-1	150
40960A	**25D6**	C.	1/4/6	2500	11-13	1400	8-10	400	0-2	200
40961A	**22D6**	C.	3/7/8	2700	13-15	1000	6.5-8.5	500	1-3	200
40961B	**22D6**	C.	3/9/6	2500	13-15	1300	7-9	400	0-2	150
40962A	**DM6**	A/C.	4/13/10	1500	12-14	900	8.5-10.5	350	0-1	250
40963A	**25D6**	C.	6/11/5	2000	7-9	850	4.5-6.5	550	1-3	325
40964A	**23D4**	C.	—	2500	14-16	1325	6-8.5	800	1-3	250
40965A	**25D6**	A/C.	4/13/10	1500	12-14	900	8.5-10.5	350	0-1	250
40966A	**25D6**	C.	5/12/8	3200	17-19	850	6.5-8.5	550	1-4	300
40967A	**25D6**	C.	5/13/10	2500	11-13	1150	7-9	600	1-3	350
40967B	**25D6**	C.	5/13/10	2800	12-14	1150	7-9	600	1-3	350
40968A	**25D4**	C.	3/8/7	2800	16-18	950	709	300	0-1	200
40969A	**25D4**	C.	3/10/10	2800	11-13	1000	4.5-6.5	350	0-1	250
40970A	**25D4**	C.	5/12/8	3200	18-20	1000	6.5-8.5	500	0.5-2.5	250

Service No.	Model	Rotation	Vacuum Code	Run up to (Rev/ Min)	Advance to be (Degrees)	Intermediate Advance I (Rev/ Min)	I (Degrees)	II (Rev/ Min)	II (Degrees)	No advance Below (Rev/ Min)
40971A	**25D6**	C.	–	1200	6.5-8.5	800	3.5-5.5	700	0.5-2.5	600
40973A	**25D6**	C.	4/15/8	2500	14-16	1100	9.5-11.5	400	1-3	175
40974A	**25D4**	C.	4/8/5	2800	20-22	1300	12-14	450	1-3	250
40975A	**25D6**	C.	5/13/10	2800	14-16	1250	10-12	550	1-3	300
40976A	**25D6**	C.	4/13/10	2800	13-15	1200	9-11	600	1.5-3.5	325
40977A	**25D6**	C.	4/15/7	2600	10-12	700	5-7	500	1-3	350
40978A	**25D4**	C.	4/8/5	2600	13-15	1150	5-7	350	0-1	200
40979A	**23D4**	C.	–	3800	14-16	800	5-7	300	0-1.5	225
40980A	**22D6**	C.	7/14/8	2300	8.5-10.5	1250	6.5-8.5	650	2-4	300
40981A	**DMBZ6**	C.	–	1500	8-10	750	4.5-6.5	500	1-3	275
40982A	**DZS4A**	C.	–	1800	9-11	1000	5.5-7.5	500	1-3	180
40983A	**25D4**	C.	5/16/12	3000	14.5-16.5	1500	8-10	800	0.5-2.5	575
40984A	**25D4**	C.	5/17/10	2800	13.5-15.5	1600	9.5-11.5	700	1-3	550
40985A	**23D4**	C.	–	3500	11-13	1000	7-9	450	0-2	200
40986A	**25D4**	C.	5/17/9	2500	13.5 max.	1250	8-10	650	1-3	400
40987A	**25D4**	C.	5/17/9	2800	11 max.	1000	5-7	600	0-2	400
40988A	**25D6**	C.	4/12/9	3000	12 max.	950	5.5-7.5	600	1-3	375
40989A	**25D6**	C.	5/17/9	3000	10 max.	900	5.5-7.5	400	1-3	325
40990A	**25D4**	C.	4/7/7	1500	9-11	900	5.5-8	650	0-2.5	525
40991A	**25D6**	C.	5/11/7	2000	9-11	650	4-6	400	0.5-2.5	225
40992A	**25D4**	C.	4/14/8	2200	13-15	1400	10-12	600	1.5-4	400
40993A	**23D6**	C.	–	Locked Mechanism						

40994A	**25D6**	C.	5/20/12	2000	7-9	1600	6-8	900	1-3	400
40995A	**25D6**	C.	6/11/5	2000	10-12	1075	5-7	575	0.5-2.5	300
40996A	**25D6**	C.	9/24/8	1600	18-20	725	9-12	325	1-4	100
40997A	**25D6**	C.	5/12/8	1500	11-13	650	6-8	300	0.5-2.5	150
40998A	**25D6**	C.	6/11/5	2000	12-14	925	6-8	525	1-3	300
40999A	**25D6**	C.	4/13/12	2600	17-19	800	8.5-10.5	400	0-3	275
41000A	**25D6**	A/C.	6/14/8	2200	11-13	500	3-5	300	0-2	225
41001A	**25D6**	C.	5/9/4(y)	2000	10-12	1075	5-7	575	0.5-2.5	300
41002A	**25D6**	A/C.	5/17/9	2000	9-11	925	5-7	700	3-5	250
41003A	**25D6**	C.	6/17/9(z)	2500	11.5-13	1150	8-10	500	3.5-6.5	300
41004A	**25D4**	C.	7/14/10(z)	2500	16-18.5	1200	6.5-9	750	1-3.5	450
41005A	**25D6**	C.	5/12/8(z)	1500	11-13	500	7-9	300	1.5-4.5	150
41006A	**25D6**	C.	3/15/9(z)	2500	15 max.	1300	11.5-13.5	700	6.5-9.5	300
41007A	**25D4**	C.	5/11/8(z)	3000	13 max.	1950	7.5-9.5	850	0.5-2.5	425
41008A	**22D6**	C.	7/14/8(z)	2000	10-12	850	7-9	450	0-2.5	325
41009A	**22D6**	C.	4/18/12(z)	2800	9-11	1450	5-7	650	1-3	50
41010A	**22D6**	C.	8/18/7(z)	3400	19 max.	1300	10-12	500	1-3	250
41011A	**22D6**	C.	4/17/6(z)	2800	19-21	1150	8-10	450	1-3	100
41012A	**22D6**	C.	4/13/10(z)	2000	13-15	1400	12-14	550	2.5-4.5	225
41013A	**22D6**	C.	4/18/12(z)	2800	19-21	1200	7-9	525	0-2	325
41014A	**22D6**	C.	5/12/8(z)	2000	13 max.	1100	8-10	550	2.5-4.5	225
41015A	**22D6**	C.	3/13/12(z)	3200	13-15	2150	11-13	800	5-7	160
41016A	**22D6**	C.	7/18/12(z)	2000	13-15	1050	6-8	650	1-3	400
41017A	**22D6**	C.	4/18/12	2500	13-15	1200	7-9	300	0-1.5	175
41018A	**22D6**	C.	4/17/6(z)	2000	6-7.5	1000	5-7	450	0.5-2.5	150
41019A	**22D6**	C.	7/14/8(z)	2300	8.5-10.5	800	5-7	650	2-4	400
41020A	**22D6**	C.	4/17/6(z)	2000	7-9	1000	5-7	450	0.5-2.5	150

Service No.	Model	Rotation	Vacuum Code	Run up to (Rev/ Min)	Advance to be (Degrees)	Intermediate Advance I (Rev/ Min)	Intermediate Advance I (Degrees)	Intermediate Advance II (Rev/ Min)	Intermediate Advance II (Degrees)	No advance Below (Rev/ Min)
41021A	**22D6**	C.	4/18/12(z)	2400	11-13	1500	9-11	450	0.5-2.5	150
41022A	**22D6**	C.	3/13/12(z)	3200	20-23	1100	11-13	450	0.5-3.5	300
41023A	**25D4**	C.	4/8/5	2000	9-11	900	4.5-6.5	500	1-3	150
41024A	**23D4**	C.	—	3300	13-15	2400	10-12	950	2-4	250
41025A	**25D4**	C.	5/17/10(z)	2800	16-18	1250	7-9	600	0.5-2.5	250
41026A	**25D4**	C.	7/13/5(z)	2200	17 max.	1250	12-14	350	0.5-2.5	250
41027A	**25D4**	C.	6/13/7(z)	3200	15-17	1250	8-10	400	0.5-2.5	100
41028A	**25D4**	C.	4/7/7(z)	2500	14-16	850	6.5-8.5	500	1.5-5.5	250
41029A	**25D4**	C.	3/13/12(z)	3000	17-19	1500	8.5-10.5	550	0.5-2.5	250
41030A	**25D4**	C.	5/11/7(z)	2800	11-13	1700	8-10	450	0-2.5	300
41031A	**25D4**	C.	3/7/8(z)	3300	16 max.	900	8-10	500	1.5-4.5	200
41032A	**25D4**	C.	3/8/7(z)	3300	15-17	900	6-8	400	0.5-2.5	150
41033A	**23D4**	C.	—	3800	14-16	800	5-7	300	0-1.5	225
41034A	**25D4**	C.	7/18/12(y)	2800	11-13	1000	4.5-6.5	350	0-1	250
41034F	**25D4**	C.	3/10/10(y)	2800	11-13	1000	4.5-6.5	350	0-1	250
41035A	**25D4**	C.	5/12/8	3200	18-20	1000	6.5-8.5	500	0.5-2.5	250
41036A	**25D4**	C.	3/7/8(z)	2000	14-16	1300	11-13	600	0.5-2.5	400
41037A	**23D4**	C.	—	2800	13.5-15.5	1400	7.5-9.5	650	0-1	575
41038A	**23D4**	C.	—	2300	12-14	700	4-6	400	0-2	300
41039A	**25D4**	C.	4/14/8(z)	2000	17-19	850	8-10	450	1-3	250
41040A	**25D4**	C.	3/8/7(z)	2500	11-13	600	6-8	350	1-3	200
41041A	**25D4**	C.	5/14/11(z)	2500	16-18	1100	8-10	475	1-3	220

41042A	**25D4**	C.	5/14/11(y)	2500	16-18	1100	8-10	475	1-3	220
41043A	**25D4**	C.	5/11/7(y)	3000	16-18	1300	9-11	400	0.5-3.5	250
41044A	**25D4**	C.	4/8/5(y)	3300	13-15	2400	10-12	950	2-4	250
41045A	**25D4**	C.	4/8/5(y)	2700	13-15	600	8-10.5	300	0-3	175
41046A	**25D4**	A/C.	5/14/11(y)	2200	15-17	950	6-8	475	0-2	300
41047A	**25D4**	A/C.	6/14/8(y)	2000	18 max.	1000	10-12	400	2-6	200
41048A	**25D4**	A/C.	8/18/7(z)	2000	20-23	800	9-11.5	450	1-4	280
41049A	**25D6**	C.	8/18/7(y)	1200	9-11	600	5-7	350	0-2	225
41050A	**25D6**	C.	2/6/3(y)	1800	14-16	750	6-8	400	0.5-2.5	230
41051A	**25D6**	C.	9/24/8(y)	1500	11-13	800	8-11	370	0-3	200
41052A	**25D6**	C.	6/14/8(z)	2400	14-16	1100	7.5-9.5	450	1-3	175
41053A	**25D6**	C.	4/7/8(y)	1500	11-13	650	6-8	300	0.5-2.5	150
41054A	**25D6**	C.	6/14/8(z)	1500	13-15	600	6-8	400	1.5-4	225
41055A	**25D4**	C.	3/8/7(z)	2500	11-13	600	6-8	350	1-3	200
41056A	**23D4**	C.	—	3300	13-15	2400	10-12	950	2-4	250
41057A	**25D4**	C.	7/13/8(z)	2800	13-15	1150	8-10	450	0.5-2.5	200
41058A	**25D4**	C.	3/10/10(y)	3300	15-17	1000	9-11	300	0-1	250
41059A	**22D4**	C.	3/10/10(y)	2700	10-12	1100	6-8	450	0.5-2.5	250
41060A	**22D6**	C.	7/14/8(y)	2300	8.5-10.5	800	5-7	525	0-1.5	300
41061A	**22D6**	C.	5/14/11(y)	3500	24-26	1400	15-17	500	1-3	200
41062A	**22D6**	C.	3/13/12(y)	3200	20-23	1700	14-16	600	3.5-6.5	200
41063A	**22D6**	C.	8/18/7(y)	3400	19 max.	1300	10-12	500	1-3	200
41064A	**22D6**	C.	5/12/8(y)	2000	13 max.	800	6-8	400	0.5-2.5	225
41065A	**22D6**	C.	7/14/8(y)	2300	8.5-10.5	1250	6.5-8.5	650	2-4	300
41066A	**23D4**	C.	—	2800	13.5-15.5	1100	7.5-9	700	1-3	550
41067A	**23D4**	C.	—	2800	11 max.	1000	5-7	600	0-2	400
41068A	**23D6**	C.	—	3000	10 max.	900	5.5-7.5	400	0-1	325

Service No.	Model	Rotation	Vacuum Code	Run up to (Rev/Min)	Advance to be (Degrees)	Intermediate Advance I (Rev/Min)	I (Degrees)	II (Rev/Min)	II (Degrees)	No advance Below (Rev/Min)
41021A	**22D6**	C.	4/18/12(z)	2400	11-13	1500	9-11	450	0.5-2.5	150
41022A	**22D6**	C.	3/13/12(z)	3200	20-23	1100	11-13	450	0.5-3.5	300
41023A	**25D4**	C.	4/8/5	2000	9-11	900	4.5-6.5	500	1-3	150
41024A	**23D4**	C.	—	3300	13-15	2400	10-12	950	2-4	250
41025A	**25D4**	C.	5/17/10(z)	2800	16-18	1250	7-9	600	0.5-2.5	250
41026A	**25D4**	C.	7/13/5(z)	2200	17 max.	1250	12-14	350	0.5-2.5	250
41027A	**25D4**	C.	6/13/7(z)	3200	15-17	1250	8-10	400	0.5-2.5	100
41028A	**25D4**	C.	4/7/7(z)	2500	14-16	850	6.5-8.5	500	1.5-5.5	250
41029A	**25D4**	C.	3/13/12(z)	3000	17-19	1500	8.5-10.5	550	0.5-2.5	250
41030A	**25D4**	C.	5/11/7(z)	2800	11-13	1700	8-10	450	0-2.5	300
41031A	**25D4**	C.	3/7/8(z)	3300	16 max.	900	8-10	500	1.5-4.5	200
41032A	**25D4**	C.	3/8/7(z)	3300	15-17	900	6-8	400	0.5-2.5	150
41033A	**23D4**	C.	—	3800	14-16	800	5-7	300	0-1.5	225
41034A	**25D4**	C.	7/18/12(y)	2800	11-13	1000	4.5-6.5	350	0-1	250
41034F	**25D4**	C.	3/10/10(y)	2800	11-13	1000	4.5-6.5	350	0-1	250
41035A	**25D4**	C.	5/12/8	3200	18-20	1000	6.5-8.5	500	0.5-2.5	250
41036A	**25D4**	C.	3/7/8(z)	2000	14-16	1300	11-13	600 q	0.5-2.5	400
41037A	**23D4**	C.	—	2800	13.5-15.5	1400	7.5-9.5	650	0-1	575
41038A	**23D4**	C.	—	2300	12-14	700	4-6	400	0-2	300
41039A	**25D4**	C.	4/14/8(z)	2000	17-19	850	8-10	450	1-3	250
41040A	**25D4**	C.	3/8/7(z)	2500	11-13	600	6-8	350	1-3	200
41041A	**25D4**	C.	5/14/11(z)	2500	16-18	1100	8-10	475	1-3	220

41042A	**25D4**	C.	5/14/11(y)	2500	16-18	1100	8-10	475	1-3	220
41043A	**25D4**	C.	5/11/7(y)	3000	16-18	1300	9-11	400	0.5-3.5	250
41044A	**25D4**	C.	4/8/5(y)	3300	13-15	2400	10-12	950	2-4	250
41045A	**25D4**	C.	4/8/5(y)	2700	13-15	600	8-10.5	300	0-3	175
41046A	**25D4**	A/C.	5/14/11(y)	2200	15-17	950	6-8	475	0-2	300
41047A	**25D4**	A/C.	6/14/8(y)	2000	18 max.	1000	10-12	400	2-6	200
41048A	**25D4**	A/C.	8/18/7(z)	2000	20-23	800	9-11.5	450	1-4	280
41049A	**25D6**	C.	8/18/7(y)	1200	9-11	600	5-7	350	0-2	225
41050A	**25D6**	C.	2/6/3(y)	1800	14-16	750	6-8	400	0.5-2.5	230
41051A	**25D6**	C.	9/24/8(y)	1500	11-13	800	8-11	370	0-3	200
41052A	**25D6**	C.	6/14/8(z)	2400	14-16	1100	7.5-9.5	450	1-3	175
41053A	**25D6**	C.	4/7/8(y)	1500	11-13	650	6-8	300	0.5-2.5	150
41054A	**25D6**	C.	6/14/8(z)	1500	13-15	600	6-8	400	1.5-4	225
41055A	**25D4**	C.	3/8/7(z)	2500	11-13	600	6-8	350	1-3	200
41056A	**23D4**	C.	—	3300	13-15	2400	10-12	950	2-4	250
41057A	**25D4**	C.	7/13/8(z)	2800	13-15	1150	8-10	450	0.5-2.5	200
41058A	**25D4**	C.	3/10/10(y)	3300	15-17	1000	9-11	300	0-1	250
41059A	**22D4**	C.	3/10/10(y)	2700	10-12	1100	6-8	450	0.5-2.5	250
41060A	**22D6**	C.	7/14/8(y)	2300	8.5-10.5	800	5-7	525	0-1.5	300
41061A	**22D6**	C.	5/14/11(y)	3500	24-26	1400	15-17	500	1-3	200
41062A	**22D6**	C.	3/13/12(y)	3200	20-23	1700	14-16	600	3.5-6.5	200
41063A	**22D6**	C.	8/18/7(y)	3400	19 max.	1300	10-12	500	1-3	200
41064A	**22D6**	C.	5/12/8(y)	2000	13 max.	800	6-8	400	0.5-2.5	225
41065A	**22D6**	C.	7/14/8(y)	2300	8.5-10.5	1250	6.5-8.5	650	2-4	300
41066A	**23D4**	C.	—	2800	13.5-15.5	1100	7.5-9	700	1-3	550
41067A	**23D4**	C.	—	2800	11 max.	1000	5-7	600	0-2	400
41068A	**23D6**	C.	—	3000	10 max.	900	5.5-7.5	400	0-1	325

Service No.	Model	Rotation	Vacuum Code	Run up to (Rev/Min)	Advance to be (Degrees)	(Rev/Min)	Intermediate Advance I (Degrees)	(Rev/Min)	Intermediate Advance II (Degrees)	No advance Below (Rev/Min)
41069A	**31D4**	A/C.	5/15/6(y)	2500	14-16	1000	9-11	450	0.5-2.5	300
41070A	**31D4**	A/C	5/15/6(y)	2500	15-17	1000	7-9	600	1-3	400
41071A	**31D6**	A/C.	5/15 /6(y)	2500	14-16	1000	9-11	450	0.5-2.5	300
41071E	**31D6**	A/C	4/8/6(y)	3000	12-14	1500	8.5-10.5	550	0.5-2.5	300
41072A	**31D6**	A/C.	5/15/6(z)	2500	15-17	1000	7-9	600	1-3	400
41072D	**31D6**	A/C.	4/10/8(y)	2800	15-17	1300	10-12	400	0-1	300
41074A	**25D6**	C.	6/11/5(y)	2200	11.5-13.5	1100	5-7.5	700	1-3.5	300
41075A	**25D6**	C.	6/11/5(z)	2200	11.5-13.5	1100	5-7.5	700	1-3.5	300
41076A	**25D4**	C.	4/7/8	2600	14-16	1050	8-10	550	0.5-2.5	400
41077A	**25D4**	C.	4/8/5(y)	1800	12-14	1050	8-10	500	1-3	250
41078A	**23D4**	C.	—	2500	13.5 max.	1250	8-10	650	1-3	400
41079A	**23D6**	C.	—	3000	13 max.	950	5.5-7.5	600	1-3	375
41080A	**25D4**	C.	5/16/12(z)	3300	16-18	1400	11.5-13.5	550	2-4	200
41081A	**23D4**	C.	—	2800	12-14	1500	7.5-9.5	850	3-4	300
41082A	**23D4**	C.	—	2800	16-18	1250	7-9	600	0.5-2.5	250
41083A	**25D6**	C.	—	1500	8-10	750	4.5-6.5	500	1-3	275
41084A	**23D6**	C.	—	1800	14-16	1000	10-12	400	0.5-2.5	230
41085A	**25D4**	C.	4/7/6(z)	1800	9-11	850	5-7	400	1-3	250
41086A	**25D6**	C.q	8/18/7(y)	1200	9-11	600	5-7	350	0-2	225
41087A	**25D6**	C.	2/6/3(y)	1800	14-16	1000	10-12	400	0.5-2.5	230
41088A	**23D6**	A/C.	—	2500	22.75	800	6.25-8.25	350	0.5-2.5	200
41089A	**25D4**	C.	7/18/12(z)	3100	20-22	1250	6-8	750	0-1	600

41090A	**25D4**	C.	4/12/8(z)	2600	19-21	1100	11.5-13.5	350	3.5-6.5 q	150
41091A	**23D4**	C.	—	2200	11-13	980	5-7	500	0-2	315
41092A	**23D4**	C.	—	2500	9-11	1150	6-8	275	0-2	200
41093A	**25D4**	C.	—	3000	12-14	1450	6-8	550	0.5-2.5	150
41094A	**25D4**	C.	7/8/12(z)	2500	20-23	1270	13-15.5	430	4-7	200
41095A	**25D4**	A/C.	5/14/11(z)	2200	15-17	950	6-8	475	0-2	300
41096A	**25D4**	C.	3/13/12(z)	3000	17-19	1500	8.5-10.5	375	0-1	200
41097A	**25D4**	C.	5/17/10(z)	2500	14-16	1325	6-8.5	800	1-3	200
41098A	**25D4**	C.	6/14/8(z)	3000	17-19	1500	8.5-10.5	550	0.5-2	200
41099A	**25D4**	C.	3/9/8(z)	3000	15-17	1300	10-12	575	4.5-7.5	325
41100A	**25D4**	A/C.	3/6/6	1600	9-11	1200	6-9	700	1-3.5	300
41101A	**25D4**	C.	3/15/9(z)	3000	6-8	1500	3-5	1075	0.5-2.5	600
41102A	**25D4**	C.	4/17/15(z)	2800	14-16	2050	12-15	1000	0-3	550
41103A	**25D4**	C.	4/19/12(z)	2500	14-16	1325	6-8.5	500	0-1	300
41104A	**25D4**	C.	6/11/5(z)	2600	14.5-16.5	850	4-6	400	0-2	175
41105A	**25D4**	C.	7/18/8	2800	7-9	1100	2.5-4.5	250	0-1	100
41106A	**25D4**	C.	4/7/7	1100	14-16	500	8.5-10.5	250	0-3	150
41107A	**25D4**	C.	3/9/8	3200	18-20	450	6-10	325	1-5	225
41109A	**25D4**	C.	5/12/6	2800	12-14	1750	9-11	800	4-6	250
41110A	**25D4**	C.	7/14/8	1800	15 max.	950	9.5-11.5	550	0.5-3.5	400
41111A	**25D4**	A/C.	3/21/8	2600	12-14	1500	9-11	450	4.5-7	200
41112A	**23D4**	C.	—	2700	9-11	1000	4.5-6.5	450	0.5-2.5	175
41113A	**23D4**	C.	—	2600	14-16	1150	9.5-11.5	500	1.5-3.5	200
41114A	**23D4**	C.	—	2700	20-23	600	7-9	350	1-4.5	200
41115A	**23D4**	C.	—	3000	16-18	2100	14-16	650	5-7	250
41116A	**25D4**	C.	5/17/10(z)	3000	12.5-14.5	1500	8-10	700	0.5-3	575
41117A	**25D4**	A/C.	11/16/6	3000	17-19	1800	11-13	350	0.5-2.5	250

Service No.	Model	Rotation	Vacuum Code	Run up to (Rev/ Min)	Advance to be (Degrees)	(Rev/ Min)	Intermediate Advance I (Degrees)	(Rev/ Min)	II (Degrees)	No advance Below (Rev/ Min)
41118A	**23D4**	C.	—	3200	12-14	1050	8-10	650	0.5-2.5	525
41119A	**25D4**	C.	4/14/8(z)	2600	12-14	1850	10-12	550	0.5-2.5	400
41120A	**23D4**	C.	—	3300	13-15	2400	10-12	950	2-4	250
41122A	**25D4**	C.	4/14/8(y)	3000	13-15	1300	6.5-8.5	600	1-3	400
41123A	**25D4**	A/C.	2/6/3(y)	3200	9-11	1100	4-6	550	0-2	400
41124A	**25D4**	C.	5/8/3(z)	3400	11-13	1500	7.5-9.5	800	3.5-5.5	300
41125A	**25D4**	C.	4/7/8(y)	2600	16-18	1050	8.5-10.5	500	1-3	350
41126A	**23D4**	C.	—	1800	18-20	850	14-16	450	2-5	300
41127A	**25D4**	C.	5/11/8(y)	1500	6-8	850	4.5-5.5	550	0.5-2.5	300
41127B	**25D4**	C.	6/20/7(y)	1500	6-8	850	3.5-5.5	550	0.5-2.5	200
41128A	**25D6**	C.	6/20/7(y)	2600	11-13	800	6-8	450	1-3	300
41129A	**25D4**	C.	4/8/5(y)	2450	15-17	1500	10-12	1000	5-7	300
41131A	**25D4**	C.	5/11/8(z)	3000	13 max.	1950	7.5-9.5	850	0.5-2.5	425
41132A	**25D4**	C.	3/10/10(y)	3500	15-17	1500	10-12	600	1-3	300
41133A	**22D6**	C.	8/18/7(z)	1200	9-11	600	5-7	350	0-2	225
41134A	**25D4**	C.	3/15/9(z)	3200	13-15	900	7.5-9.5	400	0-2	300
41135A	**23D6**	C.	—	1500	16-18	600	8-11	300	1-4	100
41136A	**25D4**	C.	5/16/12(y)	2800	13.5-15.5	1400	7.5-9.5	650	0-1	575
41137A	**25D4**	C.	5/17/10(y)	2800	13.5-15.5	1100	7.5-9.5	700	1-3	550
41138A	**23D4**	C.	—	2800	12-14	1500	7.5-9.5	850	3-5	300
41139A	**23D4**	C.	—	2800	16-18	1250	7-9	350	0-5	250
41140A	**22D6**	C.	—	1500	14 max.	800	8.5-10.5	400	1.5-3.5	200

41141A	**25D4**	C.	4/7/6(z)	1500	9-11	650	6.25-8.25	400	1.5-3.5	260
41142A	**25D4**	C.	6/13/7(z)	3000	15-17	1200	7-9	600	1-3	300
41143A	**25D4**	A/C.	8/17/7(y)	2000	20-23	800	9-11.5	450	1-4	280
41144A	**25D6**	C.	6/14/8(y)	2400	14-16	1100	7.5-9.5	450	1-3	150
41145A	**25D6**	C.	6/14/8(y)	1500	13-15	600	6-8	270	0-1	200
41146A	**25D4**	C.	6/17/7(y)	3200	12-14	1050	8-10	650	0.5-2.5	525
41147A	**25D4**	C.	6/13/7(z)	3000	15-17	1300	7-9	600	1-3	300
41148A	**25D4**	C.	5/18/3(z)	3400	11-13	1500	7.5-9.5	800	3.5-5.5	300
41149A	**25D4**	C.	7/18/12(z)	2500	16 max.	1500	9-11	450	0.5-2.5	150
41150A	**25D4**	C.	4/17/6(z)	2300	12-14	700	4-6	400	0-2	300
41151A	**25D4**	C.	4/8/5(y)	2600	16-18	1050	8.5-10.5	500	1-3	350
41152A	**25D4**	C.	5/17/10(z)	1800	13-15	1000	10.5-12.5	300	0-2.5	150
41153A	**23D4**	C.	Locked Auto-Advance Mechanism							
41154A	**25D4**	C.	6/16/12(z)	2300	12-14	1350	8.5-20.5	400	0-2	300
41155A	**25D4**	C.	5/13/10(z)	1500	9-11	450	3.5-5.5	300	0-3	200
41156A	**25D4**	C.	4/12/8(z)	2500	11-13	500	3.5-5.5	300	0-3	200
41147A	**25D4**	C.	7/18/12(z)	1800	9-11	1000	5.5-7.5	500	1-3	180
41158A	**25D4**	C.	4/14/8(z)	2000	17-19	850	8-10	450	1-3	250
41159A	**25D4**	C.	6/16/12(z)	2000	18-20	1100	8-11	675	0-3	400
41160A	**25D4**	C.	4/13/12(z)	2500	16-18	1100	8-10	475	1-3	220
41161A	**25D4**	C.	4/13/10(z)	2750	15-17	900	7-9	400	0-0.5	330
41162A	**DZS4A**	C.	—	2700	21 max.	1250	11-13	450	2-6	225
41163A	**25D6**	C.	5/8/3(y)	2800	11-13	850	6.5-8.5	450	0-2	300
41164A	**DW13A6**	A/C.	—	2200	16-18	900	11-13	450	1-3	300
41165A	**25D4**	C.	7/18/12(z)	2500	16 max.	1500	9-11	450	0.5-2.5	150
41166A	**25D6**	C.	5/13/10(y)	2800	12-14	1150	7-9	450	0-1	350
41167A	**25D6**	C.	5/13/10(y)	2800	14-16	1250	10-12	550	1-3	300

Service No.	Model	Rotation	Vacuum Code	Run up to (Rev/Min)	Advance to be (Degrees)	Intermediate Advance I (Rev/Min)	I (Degrees)	II (Rev/Min)	II (Degrees)	No advance Below (Rev/Min)
41168A	**22D6**	C.	6/18/10(y)	3200	8-10	1150	4-6	525	0.5-2.5	250
41169A	**25D6**	A/C.	4/13/10(z)	3000	11-13	1000	6.5-8.5	500	1.5-3.5	200
41170A	**25D4**	C.	4/7/8(y)	2500	19-21	800	11-13	400	0-1	300
41170B	**25D4**	C.	4/7/8(y)	2800	18-20	1000	10-12	500	1.5-3.5	350
41171A	**25D6**	C.	4/18/12(z)	2500	15-17	1000	11.5-13.5	450	0-1	350
41172A	**25D6**	C.	4/17/6(z)	2500	11-13	1150	7-9	600	1-3	350
41173A	**25D4**	C.	4/14/8(z)	2600	12-14	1850	10-12	550	0.5-2.5	400
41174A	**25D4**	C.	3/7/8(z)	2000	14-16	1300	11-13	600	0.5-2.5	400
41175A	**20D8**	C.	6/17/9(z)	2800	10.5-12.5	900	7-9	500	0-3	350
41176A	**35D8**	A/C.	5/17/8(y)	2800	12-14	900	6-18	500	1-3	300
41177A	**25D4**	C.	4/8/5(y)	2800	13-15	1200	9-11	600	1.5-3.5	300
41180A	**23D4**	C.	—	2500	12 max.	1500	8-10	600	2-4	200
41181A	**25D4**	C.	3/13/12(z)	3000	12-14	1900	10-12	350	0-2	150
41182A	**22D6**	C.	5/13/10(y)	2800	14-16	1250	10-12	550	1-3	300
41183A	**25D4**	C.	4/8/5(y)	2600	13-15	800	7-9	450	0-2	350
41186A	**25D4**	A/C.	2/6/3(y)	3200	9-11	1100	4-6	550	0-2	400
41187A	**25D4**	C.	6/13/7(y)	3000	15-17	1000	7-9	400	0-1.5	275
41188A	**25D4**	C.	3/13/12(z)	3000	12-14	1900	10-12	550	1-3	150
41189A	**23D4**	C.	—	3250	6-8	1000	4-6	600	0-2	400
41190A	**25D4**	C.	3/10/10(y)	3400	16-18	1000	8-10	400	0-1	300
41191A	**25D4**	C.	4/13/10(y)	2600	11-13	1200	8-10	600	0.5-2.5	400
41192A	**25D4**	C.	4/7/6(z)	1800	9-11	850	5-7	400	1-3	250
41193A	**25D4**	C.	4/7/6(z)	1500	9-11	650	6.25-8.25	400	1.5-3.5	260

41194A	**25D4**	A/C.	7/14/10(y)	2800	15-17	1200	9-11	350	0-1.5	250
41195A	**23D4**	C.	—	2000	9-11	900	4.5-6.5	275	0-1	100
41196A	**23D4**	C.	—	3000	12-14	1800	8-10	650	0-1	500
41196B	**23D4**	C.	—	3000	11-13	850	7-9	600	2-5.5	450
41197A	**25D4**	C.	3/10/10(z)	2500	16 max.	1500	9-11	450	0.5-2.5	150
41198A	**25D4**	C.	5/8/3(z)	2800	10-12	1150	6-8	400	1-3	250
41199A	**25D4**	C.	4/7/6(y)	2500	14-16	900	10-12	600	2-5	450
41199B	**25D4**	C.	4/7/6(y)	2500	14-16	900	10-12	600	3-6	400
41200A	**25D4**	C.	4/14/8(y)	2800	17-19	1450	13-15	650	5-9	375
41200B	**25D4**	C.	4/14/8(y)	2800	17-19	1450	13-15	600	3-6	400
41201A	**25D6**	C.	2/6/3/(z)	3000	13-15	600	6-8	350	0-3	250
41202A	**22D6**	C.	5/18/10(y) 3/8/5R(y)	2800	12-14	1150	7-9	450	0-1	350
41203A	**20D8**	C.	—	2000	17-19	1200	14-16	350	1-3	200
41204A	**25D4**	C.	3/10/10(z)	2500	16 max.	1500	9-11	450	0.5-2.5	150
41206A	**25D4**	C.	4/14/8(y)	3000	13-15	1300	6.5-8.5	600	1-3	400
41207A	**22D6**	C.	—	2600	16-18	800	8.5-10.5	400	0-1	300
41208A	**22D6**	C.	5/17/10(y)	1600	10-12	850	7.5-9.5	400	0.5-2.5	250
41209A	**25D4**	C.	7/18/12(z)	2000	9-11	700	5-7	350	0-2	250
41210A	**25D4**	C.	6/13/5(z)	1800	14-16	600	7.5-10	350	0-3	250
41211A	**25D4**	C.	5/8/3(z)	2400	14-16	1100	9-11	500	1.5-3.5	200
41212A	**25D4**	C.	4/14/8(y)	2500	11-13	700	7-10.5	500	0-3.5	350
41213A	**25D4**	C.	5/11/7(y)	2800	11-13	700	5.5-7.5	500	1.5-3.5	300
41214A	**25D4**	C.	3/10/10(z)	2500	9-11	1400	5.5-7.5	400	0-1.5	150
41215A	**25D4**	C.	3/10/10(z)	2500	9-11	1400	5.5-7.5	400	0-1.5	150
41216A	**25D4**	C.	4/7/6(y)	1800	9-11	1000	6-8	400	1-3	250
41217A	**25D4**	C.	4/7/69y)	1500	9-11	650	6.25-8.25	400	1.5-3.5	260
41218A	**25D6**	C.	2/6/3(z)	3000	13-15	1300	8-10	450	3-6	250

Service No.	Model	Rotation	Vacuum Code	Run up up to (Rev/Min)	Advance to be (Degrees)	(Rev/Min)	Intermediate Advance I (Degrees)	(Rev/Min)	II (Degrees)	No advance Below (Rev/Min)
41219B	**22D6**	C.	—	2000	6-8	1300	6-8	450	0-2	175
41220A	**25D4**	C.	5/11/8(z)	2600	14-16	1000	8010	500	0.5-2.5	350
41221A	**23D4**	C.	—	3200	12-14	900	5.5-7.5	650	0.5-2.5	525
41222A	**23D4**	C.	—	3800	14-16	800	5-7	300	0-1.5	225
41223A	**25D4**	A/C.	4/7/6(y)	3000	15-17	950	7.5-9.5	450	0-1.5	350
41224A	**25D6**	C.	5/8/3(y)	2600	14-16	950	9.5-12	400	0-1	350
41225A	**25D4**	C.	2/4/3(y)	3250	6-8	1000	4-6	600	0-2	400
41226A	**25D4**	C.	3/9/8(y)	3000	15-17	950	7.5-9.5	450	0-1.5	350
41227A	**25D6**	C.	4/17/6(y)	2500	15-17	1000	11.5-13.5	500	0-2	300
41228A	**25D6**	C.	4/17/6(y)	2000	9-11	950	6-8	400	0.5-2.5	150
41229A	**25D4**	C.	5/8/3(z)	2800	12-14	1150	6-8	400	1-3	250
41230A	**25D4**	C.	3/18/7(y)	2500	10 max.	1250	5-7	450	0.5-2.5	120
41231A	**25D4**	C.	4/13/12(y)	2000	16 max.	1050	7-9	450	0-1	370
41233A	**25D4**	C.	6/16/12(z)	2800	14-16	1500	9-11	600	2-4	300
41234A	**25D4**	C.	4/12/8(y)	3000	14-16	1600	9-11	600	1-3	250
41236A	**25D6**	C.	—	2000	6-8	800	2.5-4.5	450	0-2	175
41236B	**25D6**	C.	—	3000	9-11	1500	6-8	650	2-4	375
41237A	**25D4**	C.	5/11/7(y) 4/8/6R(y)	2800	16-18	1400	10-12	650	3-6	400
41238A	**25D4**	C.	4/11/7(y)	3000	11-13	1400	7-9	500	2-4	200
41239A	**23D4**	C.	—	3000	12-14	900	6.5-8.5	400	1-3	250
41240A	**25D4**	C.	4/18/12(z)	2500	22-24	1050	14-16	600	3.5-7	400
41241A	**22D4**	C.	—	2000	15-17	950	11-13	400	1-3	250

41241B	**22D4**	C.	—	1800	11-13	1000	7.5-9.5	700	2.5-4.5	450
41242A	**25D4**	C.	3/15/9(y)	3200	13-15	1400	9-11	400	0-2	300
41243A	**23D4**	C.	—	1500	11-13	900	10-11	300	0.5-2.5	150
41244A	**25D4**	C.	7/14/10(y)	2800	15-17	1200	9-11	500	2-4	250
41245A	**25D4**	C.	4/7/6(y)	2500	9-11	1500	7-9	700	0.5-2.5	400
41245B	**25D4**	C.	4/5/5(y)	2500	9-11	1500	7-9	700	0.5-2.5	400
41246A	**25D4**	C.	6/14/8(y)	3000	10-12	1200	4.5-6.5	450	0-0.5	400
41247A	**25D6**	A/C.	4/8/5(y)	1500	8-10	750	4.5-6.5	500	1-3	275
41248A	**25D4**	C.	2/5/5(y)	2400	7-9	1450	5-7	500	0-2	200
41249A	**25D4**	C.	7/13/5(y)	2200	17 max.	1250	12-14	450	4.5-7.5	250
41250A	**25D4**	C.	5/11/8(y)	3000	13 max.	1950	7.5-9.5	850	0.5-2.5	425
41251A	**25D4**	C.	3/15/9(y)	3200	13-15	1400	9-11	400	0-2	300
41252A	**25D4**	C.	5/11/8(y)	3000	13 max.	1950	7.5-9.5	850	0.5-2.5	425
41253A	**25D4**	C.	5/16/12(y)	3300	16-18	1400	11.5-13.5	550	2-4	200
41254A	**25D4**	C.	5/11/7(y)	2800	11-13	1700	8-10	650	3-5	300
41255A	**25D4**	C.	3/8/7(y)	3300	15-17	1450	10-12	400	0.5-2.5	150
41256A	**25D4**	C.	3/7/8(y)	3300	16 max.	1100	11-13	500	1.5-4.5	200
41257A	**25D4**	C.	3/10/10(y)	2500	9-11	1400	5.5-7.5	400	0-1.5	150
41258A	**25D4**	C.	3/10/10(y)	2500	9-11	1400	5.5-7.5	400	0-1.5	150
41259A	**25D4**	C.	6/16/12(y)	2800	14-16	1500	9-11	600	2-4	300
41260A	**25D4**	C.	6/13/7(y)	3000	15-17	1700	10-12	600	1-3	300
41261A	**25D4**	C.	3/13/12(y)	3000	12-14	1550	9-11	350	0-2	150
41262A	**25D4**	C.	5/17/10(y)	2800	16-18	1250	7-9	600	0.5-2.5	250
41263A	**25D4**	C.	5/8/3(y)	3400	11-13	1500	7.5-9.5	500	0-2	300
41264A	**25D4**	C.	5/11/8(y)	2600	14-16	1150	9-11	500	0.5-2.5	350
41265A	**25D4**	C.	4/7/7(y)	2500	14-16	1150	8-10	500	1.5-3.5	250
41266A	**25D4**	C.	3/13/12(y)	3000	12-14	1550	9-11	350	0-2	150

Service No.	Model	Rotation	Vacuum Code	Run up to (Rev/Min)	Advance to be (Degrees)	Intermediate Advance I (Rev/Min)	Intermediate Advance I (Degrees)	Intermediate Advance II (Rev/Min)	Intermediate Advance II (Degrees)	No advance Below (Rev/Min)
41267A	**25D4**	C.	3/8/7(y)	2500	11-13	1200	8-10	650	0.5-2.5	450
41268A	**23D4**	C.	–	2000	9-11	1250	7-9	450	0.5-2.5	150
41269A	**25D4**	C.	5/8/3(y)	3400	11-13	1500	7.5-9.5	500	0-2	300
41270A	**25D4**	C.	5/8/3(y)	2800	10-12	1150	6-8	400	1-3	250
41271A	**25D4**	C.	5/8/3(y)	2800	12-14	1150	6-8	400	1-3	250
41273A	**22D6**	C.	2/10/12(y)	2500	12 max.	1500	8-10	600	2-4	200
41274A	**22D6**	C.	7/14/8(y)	2300	8.5-10.5	1250	6.5-8.5	650	2-4	300
41275A	**25D6**	C.	7/14/10(y)	2500	10-12	1250	7-9	400	1-3.5	250
41276A	**35D8**	C.	6/20/7(y)	3200	12-14	1700	8-10	600	0-2	350
41277D	**35D8**	A/C.	2/4/4R(y)	2800	12-14	1200	7-9	600	1.5-3	350
41277E	**35D8**	A/C.	2/5/5R(y)	2800	12-14	1200	7-9	600	1.5-3	350
41278A	**35D8**	A/C.	5/17/8(y)	2800	12-14	1900	10-12	700	4-6	300
41279A	**25D4**	C.	7/18/12(y)	2500	16 max.	1500	9-11	450	0.5-2.5	150
41280A	**25D4**	C.	7/18/12(y)	2500	16 max.	1500	9-11	450	0.5-2.5	150
41281A	**25D4**	C.	4/17/6(y)	2300	12-14	1350	8.5-10.5	500	2-4	300
41282A	**25D4**	C.	4/17/6(y)	2300	12-14	1350	8.5-10.5	500	2-4	300
41283A	**25D4**	C.	6/16/12(y)	2300	12-14	1350	8.5-10.5	500	2-4	300
41284A	**25D4**	C.	6/16/12(y)	2300	12-14	1350	8.5-10.5	500	2-4	300
41285A	**25D4**	C.	4/14/8(y)	2000	17-19	1000	9.5-11.5	450	1-3	250
41286A	**25D4**	C.	4/14/8(y)	2000	17-19	1000	9.5-11.5	450	1-3	250
41287A	**25D4**	C.	5/13/10(y)	1500	9-11	800	6.5-8.5	300	0-3	200
41288A	**25D4**	C.	5/13/10(y)	1500	9-11	800	6.5-8.5	300	0-3	200

41289A	**25D4**	C.	4/12/8(y)	2500	11-13	1050	6-8	300	0-3	200
41290A	**25D4**	C.	4/12/8(y)	2500	11-13	1050	6-8	300	0-3	200
41291A	**25D4**	C.	4/8/5(y)	2600	13-15	1200	9-11	450	0-1.5	300
41292A	**25D4**	C.	5/11/8(y)	3000	13 max.	1950	7.5-9.5	850	0.5-2.5	425
41293A	**25D4**	C.	5/16/12(y)	3300	16-18	1400	11.5-13.5	550	2-4	200
41294A	**23D6**	C.	Locked Auto-Advance Mechanism							
41295A	**25D6**	C.	5/14/11(y)	3400	13-15	1550	8-10	600	1.5-3.5	300
41296A	**22D6**	C.	—	2600	14-16	1250	11-13	600	4-6	300
41297A	**22D6**	C.	—	2600	14-16	1250	11-13	600	4-6	300
41298A	**35D8**	A/C.	2/11/7(y)	2800	12-14	1900	10-12	700	4-6	300
41299A	**22D4**	C.	5/10/6(y)	2800	10-12	1350	6-8	600	0-2	400
41300B	**35D8**	C.	13/19/8(z)	2000	17-19	1200	14-16	600	7-9	200
41300D	**35D8**	C.	4/12/9R(y)	2000	17-19	1200	14-16	600	7-9	200
41300E	**35D8**	C.	4/12/9R(y)	2250	17-19	1150	10-12	450	2.5-5	250
41301B	**25D4**	C.	5/11/7(y) 1/5/6R(y)	3000	15-17	1700	11-13	700	4-6	350
41301D	**25D4**	C.	8/24/6(y) 1/5/6R(y)	3000	15-17	1700	11-13	700	4-6	350
41302A	**25D4**	C.	5/11/7(y)	3200	15-17	2200	13-15	900	7-9	200
41302D	**25D4**	C.	5/14/11(y)	3000	15-17	1700	11-13	550	3-5	200
41303A	**25D4**	C.	4/14/8(y)	2800	14-16	1800	14-16	600	2-4	200
41304A	**25D4**	C.	5/11/7(y)	3200	15-17	2200	13-15	900	7-9	200
41304B	**25D4**	C.	5/11/7(y)	3000	15-17	1700	11-13	600	3-5	250
41305A	**22D6**	C.	2/10/12(y)	2500	12 max.	1500	8-10	600	2-4	200
41306A	**22D6**	C.	4/7/8(y) 3/10/8R(y)	3000	9-11	1500	6-8	650	2-4	375
41307A	**25D4**	C.	8/20/8(y)	2600	12-14	1850	10-12	700	3.5-5.5	400

Service No.	Model	Rotation	Vacuum Code	Run up to (Rev/Min)	Advance to be (Degrees)	Intermediate Advance I (Rev/Min)	I (Degrees)	II (Rev/Min)	II (Degrees)	No advance Below (Rev/Min)
41308A	**25D4**	C.	3/7/8(y)	2000	14-16	1300	11-13	600	0.5-2.5	400
41309A	**25D4**	C.	4/7/6(y)	2000	9-11	1000	6-8	650	3.5-6	350
41310A	**25D4**	C.	4/7/6(y)	2000	9-11	750	6-8.5	500	0-2	350
41311A	**35D8**	C.	4/7/6.5(y)	3250	9-11	1000	8-11	600	0-3	450
41311B	**35D8**	C.	5/9/5R(y)	3250	9-11	1000	8-11	600	0-3	450
41313A	**23D4**	C.	—	3600	8-10	2600	5-7	900	0-2	300
41314A	**25D6**	C.	2/7/10(y)	2800	11-13	1900	9-11	900	3-5	450
41315A	**25D4**	C.	4/18/12(z)	2800	21-23	1100	12-14	550	2-5	350
41316A	**25D4**	C.	8/20/8(y)	2800	17-19	1450	13-15	750	8-11	400
41317B	**35D8**	A/C.	5/17/8(y)	2800	12-14	1900	10-12	700	4-6	300
41318D	**35D8**	A/C.	2/4/4R(y)	2800	12-14	1200	7-9	600	1.5-3	350
41318E	**35D8**	A/C.	2/5/5R(y)	2800	12-14	1200	7-9	600	1.5-3	350
41319A	**25D4**	C.	4/7/6(y) 1/4/5R(y)	2000	9-11	1000	6-8	650	3.5-6	350
41319B	**25D4**	C.	4/7/6(y) 1/4/5R(y)	2000	9-11	1000	6-8	600	0.5-3	450
41320A	**22D6**	C.	—	2800	13-15	1050	12-15	650	2-5	450
41320E	**22D6**	C.	—	1500	8-10	1000	8-10	500	1-3	275
41322A	**22D6**	C.	4/8/5R(y)	2800	12-14	1500	9-11	700	3-5	400
41323A	**22D6**	C.	4/8/5R(y)	2800	12-14	1500	9-11	700	3-5	400
41324A	**25D4**	C.	6/16/4(y)	2800	19-21	1200	15-17	500	5-8.5	200
41325B	**35D8**	A/C.	5/17/8(y)	2800	12-14	1900	10-12	500	1-3	300

41327A	**25D4**	C.	4/8/5(y)	2600	13-15	1200	9-11	450	0-1.5	300
41329A	**22D6**	A/C.	2/5/5(y)	2800	12-14	2300	11-13	1000	4.5-6.5	400
41330A	**23D4**	C.	—	2800	8-10	1700	6.5-8.5	750	1-3	450
41331B	**25D4**	C.	5/14/9(y)	2800	8-10	2000	6-8	300	0-1	200
41332A	**22D4**	C.	5/10/6(y) 3/10/7R(y)	2800	10.5-12.5	1300	6-8	600	0-2	400
41333A	**25D4**	C.	4/7/6(y) 1/4/5R(y)	2000	9-11	750	6-8.5	500	0-2	350
41334A	**35D8**	C.	—	2250	17-19	1150	10-12	450	2.5-5	250
41335A	**22D6**	C.	7/14/10(y)	2500	10-12	1250	7-9	400	1-3.5	250
41336A	**35D8**	C.	6/20/7(y)	3200	12-14	1700	8-10	600	0-2	350
41337A	**35D8**	C.	6/20/7(y) 1/12/8R(y)	3200	12-14	1700	8-10	800	1.5-3.5	350
41338A	**25D4**	C.	7/18/12(z)	2000	9-11	1000	6.5-8.5	500	1-3	250
41339A	**25D4**	C.	7/13/5(y)	3000	9-11	1900	8-10	900	3.5-5.5	400
41340A	**25D6**	C.	—	1500	8-10	750	4.5-6.5	500	1-3	275
41341A	**25D6**	C.	4/8/5(y)	1500	8-10	750	4.5-6.5	500	1-3	275
41342A	**22D6**	C.	7/14/8(y)	2300	8.5-10.5	1250	6.5-8.5	650	2-4	300
41343A	**22D6**	C.	4/8/5R(y)	2800	12-14	1500	9-11	700	3-5	400
41344A	**22D6**	C.	7/14/8(y)	2300	8.5-10.5	1250	6.5-8.5	650	2-4	300
41345A	**22D6**	C.	4/8/5R(y)	2800	12-14	1500	9-11	700	3-5	400
41346A	**25D4**	C.	5/14/7(y)	3000	13-15	1050	10-12	1000	4.5-6.5	450
41347A	**25D4**	C.	5/14/7(y)	2800	13-15	2300	11-13	1000	4.5-6.5	500
41348A	**25D4**	C.	5/14/7(y)	2600	13-15	1700	9-11	1000	3.5-5.5	550
41349A	**25D4**	C.	5/14/7(y)	2600	8-10	1800	7-9	1000	5-7	450
41351A	**22D6**	C.	4/7/8(y)	3000	9-11	1500	6-8	650	2-4	375
41352A	**22D6**	C.	2/4/4R(y)	2800	13-15	2200	12-14	900	6.5-9	500
41353A	**25D4**	C.	1/3/3R(y)	2600	19-21	1000	9-11	600	1.5-4	350
41355A	**25D4**	C.	5/9/7(y)	3000	13-15	2050	10-12	1000	4.5-6.5	450

Service No.	Modelq	Rotationq	Vacuum Code	Run up to (Rev/ Min)	Advance to be (Degrees)	(Rev/ Min)	Intermediate Advance I (Degrees)	(Rev/ Min)	II (Degrees)	No advance Below (Rev/ Min)
41356A	**25D4**	C.	5/9/7(y)	2600	8-10	1800	7-9	1000	5-7	450
41357A	**25D4**	C.	8/20/8(y)	3200	14-16	2200	11-13	700	5-7	200
41358A	**23D4**	C.	—	3000	14-16	1000	10.5-12.5	600	4-7	300
41359A	**35D8**	C.	5/9/5R(y)	3250	9-11	1000	8-11	600	0-3	450
41360A	**35D8**	A/C.	5/17/8(y)	2800	12-14	1900	10-12	700	4-6	300
41362A	**25D4**	C.	4/8/5(y)	3000	13-15	1850	10-12	600	3-5	200
41363A	**25D4**	C.	4/18/12(y)	2700	21 max.	1250	11-13	450	2-6	225
41364A	**25D4**	C.	5/11/7(y)	3200	12-14	1700	11-13	800	6.5-8.5	200
41365D	**25D4**	C.	5/11/7(y)	2500	12-14	1600	10.5-12.5	800	6-8	400
41366A	**25D6**	C.	5/16/8(y) 2/8/5R(y)	2800	12-14	1500	9-11	700	3-5	400
41367A	**22D6**	C.	7/14/8(y)	2800	12-14	1500	9-11	700	3-5	400
41368A	**22D6**	C.	7/14/8(y)	2800	12-14	1500	9-11	700	3-5	400
41369A	**25D4**	C.	4/9/8(y)	2800	17-19	1750	14-16	1000	6-8	250
41370B	**25D4**	C.	7/13/3(y)	2800	14-16	1400	9-11	1200	7.5-9.5	400
41371E	**25D4**	C.	5/10/5(y)	3200	17-19	1850	12.5-14.5	950	2-4	500
41372A	**23D4**	C.	—	2500	9-11	1400	5.5-7.5	800	2-4	150
41373A	**25D4**	C.	5/9/7(y)	2800	12-14	1700	11-13	850	6-8	450
41374A	**25D4**	C.	5/9/7(y)	2800	11-13	2000	10-12	1000	5-7	300
41375A	**23D4**	C.	—	2800	15-17	1200	9-11	500	2-4	250
41376A	**35D8**	C.	5/17/9(y)	2800	10-12	1500	8.5-10.5	500	0-3	350
41378A	**25D6**	C.	5/10/6(y)	2800	8-10	1800	7-9	900	3-5	250

41379A	**35D8**	C.	4/12/9(y)	2250	17-19	1150	10-12	450	2.5-5	250
41380A	**35D8**	C.	—	2250	17-19	1150	10-12	450	2.5-5	250
41381A	**25D4**	C.	5/12/6(y)	2800	7-9	1400	5-7	600	0.5-2.5	450
41381B	**25D4**	C.	5/12/6(y)	2500	7-9	1000	4-6	550	1-3	300
41382A	**35D8**	A/C.	5/17/8(y) 2/8/6R(y)	2800	12-14	1200	7-9	600	1.5-3	350
41382B	**35D8**	A/C.	5/17/8(y) 2/8/6R(y)	2800	11-13	1200	5-7	900	3-5	400
41383A	**35DE8**	C.	5/9/5R(y)	3250	9-11	600	0-3	1000	8-11	300
41384A	**35D8**	C.	4/7/10R(y)	3200	14-16	2100	13-15	1200	5-7	450
41385A	**22D6**	C.	3/10/7R(y)	2800	12-14	1200	6-8	650	1-3	400
41387A	**36DE12**	C.	5/8/7R(y)	400	0	1000	6-8	1300	8-10	—
(see Note 2)				2600	11-13	3500	12-14			—
41388A	**22D6**	C.	5/8/4R(y)	2800	13-15	1250	9-11	700	1-3.5	450
41389A	**25D4**	C.	5/13/10(y)	3200	17-19	1800	12-14	700	1-3	450
41390A	**25D4**	C.	4/11/7(y)	3000	11-13	1400	7-9	500	2-4	200
41391A	**25D4**	C.	4/12/8(y)	3000	14-16	2400	13-15	1100	5-7	250
41392A	**35D8**	A/C.	5/9/5(y)	2800	10-12	1300	7-9	600	1-3	300
41393A	**35D8**	A/C.	5/6/5(y)	2800	10-12	1300	7-9	600	1-3	300
41394A	**35D8**	A/C.	5/17/8(y)	2800	13-15	2000	11-13	900	4.5-7	300
41395A	**25D4**	C.	5/8/3(y)	3200	13-15	1400	9-11	800	6-8	300
41396A	**25D4**	C.	5/14/11(y)	3000	15-17	1300	9.5-11.5	850	7-9	450
41397A	**35D8**	C.	4/12/9R(y)	2800	15-17	1800	12-14	600	1.5-3.5	250
41398A	**22D6**	C.	7/14/8(y)	2800	12-14	1500	9-11	700	3-5	400

Motorsport

HOW TO START MOTOR RACING. Wally Hall. 011.9.

The author has had considerable club racing success and has passed on most of the vast experience he has gained. Ideal for anyone at all interested in beginning.

HOW TO START RALLYING. Colin Malkin. 024.0.

This famous rally driver takes the reader through all the mystiques of rally preparation. Car selection, suitability and setting up. Bodywork, lights, driving and navigation are some of the subjects dealt with. Colin co-drove the winning London to Sydney Marathon car.

HOW TO START AUTOCROSS AND RALLYCROSS. Peter Noad. 033.X.

Like the rest of the 'How to Start' series but for the increasingly popular sport of autocross/rallycross. Like the other authors Peter Noad is an experienced and successful campaigner.

MOTORCYCLE ENGINEERING 075-5 £2.25 Phil Irving

'Phil' Irving — motorcycle designer, engineer, rider, and, as 'Slide Rule', one of the best-known technical writers on motorcycling — established his reputation as a rider After the war, as Vincent's Chief Engineer, he designed and developed the Series B 'Rapide' with its renowned variants. He has designed a six-litre diesel engine for an Australian tractor and is at present engaged in the development of racing cars and high-performance equipment.

HOW TO START PRODUCTION MOTOR CYCLE RACING

030.5

Ray Knight
Ray Knight is a journalist with 10 years racing, a TT win and lap record to his credit. He passes all his experience to the enthusiast. 'A good guide to success.

THE *BARRY LEE* BOOK OF HOT ROD RACING 062.3

Barry Lee revolutionised Hot Rod Racing in 1970 and in 1971 became British Champion, as well as making successful forays to Denmark and South Africa. In his book Barry Lee shows how he built his Escort, what it's like in a hot rod race, where and when hot rod racing takes place - in fact he writes about everything that an intending competitor, a hot rod fan or spectator will want to know.

Marque tuning guides

TUNING THE MINI. Clive Trickey **001.0.**
The Mini Tuners' Bible; universally recognised as the most authoritative book on the subject. The most popular marque tuning book to be published.

MORE MINI TUNING. Clive Trickey **000.3.**
New! The second edition of the companion volume to **'Tuning the Mini'.** Updated with much more information on valve gear, carbs, camshafts and gearboxes.

TUNING STANDARD TRIUMPHS over 1300cc. **029.1.**
David Vizard
The tuning stages for Vitesses, GT6, TRs and all 2000 units from stage 1 to full race.

TUNING STANDARD TRIUMPHS up to 1300cc. **012.7.**
Richard Hudson-Evans
Essential reading for Herald, Spitfire, 1300, Standard 8 and 10 owners. Full tuning information.

TUNING VOLKSWAGENS. Peter Noad **026.7.**
An expert guide to the race and rally preparations of VWs; it covers the various types of car and their development and competition history. Includes a section on Beach Buggies.

TUNING ESCORTS AND CAPRIS. David Vizard **009.7.**
The technical editor of **'Cars and Car Conversions'** explains engine and chassis tuning procedures for both road and track.

TUNING ANGLIAS AND CORTINAS. **003.8.**
This bestseller deals with engine and chassis tuning and details the early Classic and Capri, the V4 and Twin Cam power units.

TUNING TWIN CAM FORDS. **David Vizard** **007.0.**
The stage-by-stage modifications for these engines, from 'warm' 1600s to full-race 1800s. Fully illustrated.

TUNING FOUR CYLINDER FORDS. **Paul Davies.** **059.3.**
A new edition of this very popular tuning bible for all four cylinder models from Anglia to Cortina MK III.

TUNING BMC SPORTS CARS. **Mike Garton** **004.6.**
The author, once a technical expert at British Leyland Special Tuning Department passes his wealth of experience on to the interested owner.

TUNING VIVAS AND FIRENZAS **Blydenstein & Coburn** **064.X**
Written by the country's leading experts, this is the first tuning book on these popular cars. It covers all aspects of tuning for both road and track.

TUNING V8 ENGINES. **David Vizard** **028.3.**
This book covers the principles involved for modifying a large selection of V8 engines— design trends, supercharging, assembly, part swapping, carburation etc.

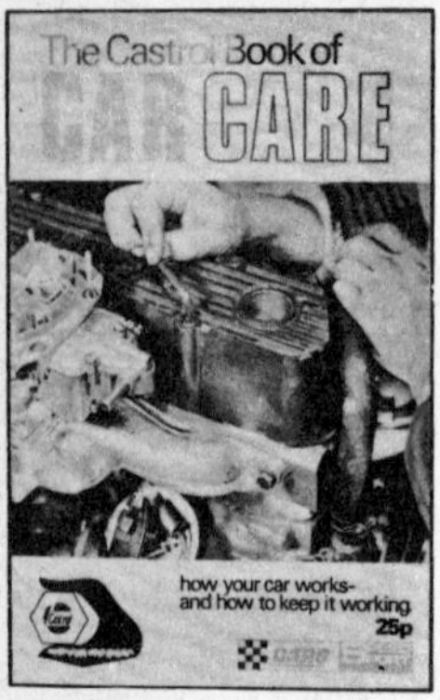

New edition Castrol Book of Car Care

SBN 902-587-005

This is the new edition of the ever popular Castrol Book of Car Care in a new format and at a new price.

Car Care' has been rewritten and considerably updated, with new drawings, diagrams and photographs. It now has a full-colour cover.

'Car Care' does exactly what its title suggests under the following chapter headings:

1. A Happy Partnership? 2. Servicing; 3. Bodywork; 4. Engine; 5. Transmission; 6. Brakes; 7. Suspension and Steering; 8. Tyres; 9. Electrics; 10. Breakdown Trouble-shooter; 11. Safety and Security; 12. Castrol at your Service.

The Big Drive

THE BIG DRIVE.
Richard Hudson-Evans and Graham Robson.
032.1.

The Book of the World Cup Rally, 1970.
The first behind-the-wheel view of the toughest rally ever—the car breaking London to Mexico Race.

Castrol Book of Motor Cycle Care

a sister publication to the **'Castrol Book of Car Care'** describes the various parts of the machine tells what they are designed to do and suggests the best course of action for looking after them. Used intelligently it can save a lot of time, money and frustration.

Still very popular and a constant best seller.

SU CARBURETTERS
ISBN: 0-903192-25-X
110 pages
One of the most informative books ever published on this popular make of carburetter. Models included are the 'H', 'HD', 'HS', 'HS8', Thermo and MC2. Extensive coverage is given to the maintenance overhaul and tuning of the SU carburetter. Also included is an application section giving carburetter details relating to vehicle make and model.
CONTENTS: Carburetter Duty — Engine Requirements — Influence of Induction Systems — SU Carburetter — Dismantling — Overhaul — Tuning — Adjusting — Servicing — Application tables, needle size charts.

STROMBERG CARBURETTERS
ISBN: 0-903192-52-7
152 pages
Full information and details of operation, testing procedure, tuning and maintenance of the Stromberg CD range of carburetters for internal combustion automobile and marine engines.

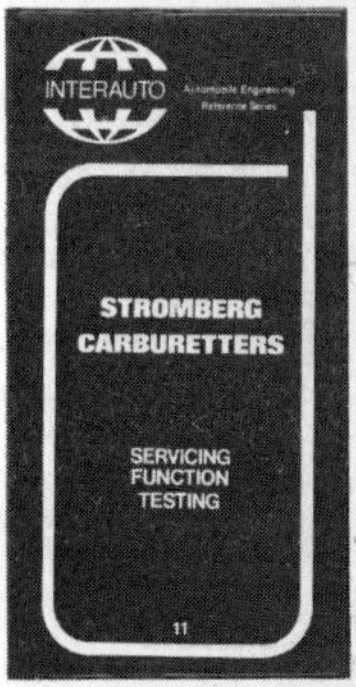

SOLEX CARBURETTERS
ISBN: 0-903192-09-8
158 pages
An informative guide with coverage of servicing, function, testing, overhauls and adjustments of French Solex models used in Citroens, Peugeots, Renaults and Simcas. With extensive data and many diagrams.

ZENITH CARBURETTERS
ISBN: 0-903192-39-X
148 pages
Like the other books in the series, gives full advice on maintenance and tells how to get the best out of your Zenith Carburetter.

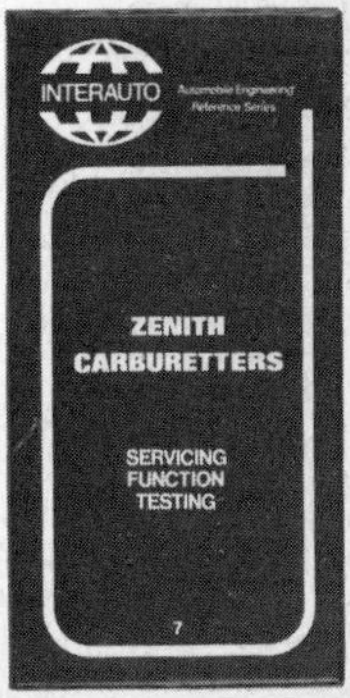

Interauto Books for the professional

Interauto Automobile Engineering Reference Series

These books are directed at the car mechanic, the apprentice, the technician and the more experienced do-it-yourself motorist. In clear language, and with numerous illustrations, each title fully details a specific motor engineering subject. All books written by leading motor engineering experts and revised in accordance with 1971/2 technologies.

Part of the series was originally published in Germany by Vogel Verlag, one of that country's largest technical publishers, who have already sold more than 100,000 copies. Licensed editions of the series are also published in Spanish and Dutch.

Each book is designed to be carried around for constant and immediate reference and its handy format facilitates this. Research with major technical booksellers has shown that no reference series of this type has previously been available and that there consequently exists an unlimited demand and sales potential. A further advantage is that the series covers a truly international selection of vehicle systems.

Current titles in this series:

Automobile Fault Diagnosis
Automobile Radio Interference Suppression
Automobile Body and Paintwork Repairs
Automobile Engine Testing
Automobile Performance Testing
Caravan Service Manual
Bosch Electrical Systems

Complete Factory Approved Service and Repair Manuals for Carburetters

SU Carburetters
Zenith Carburetters
Stromberg Carburetters
Solex Carburetters (Vol. 1 – French Solex Carburetters)

(other carburetter books are in preparation)

AUTOMOBILE BODY AND PAINTWORK REPAIRS

ISBN: 0-903192-04-7 110 pages

A concise and up-to-the-minute book dealing with a difficult and frequently under-estimated 'art'. Extensive descriptions are furnished on the various body straightening machines, welding and body finish. Also included is a section on fibreglass bodies. All body and paint repair shops will find this publication immensely helpful.
CONTENTS: Planning — Body Repairs — Body and Frame Straighteners — Straightening Techniques — Body Jigs — Body Repair Tools — Panel Beating Work — Welding — Paint Finish — Paintshop — Spraying Equipment — Paint Build-up.

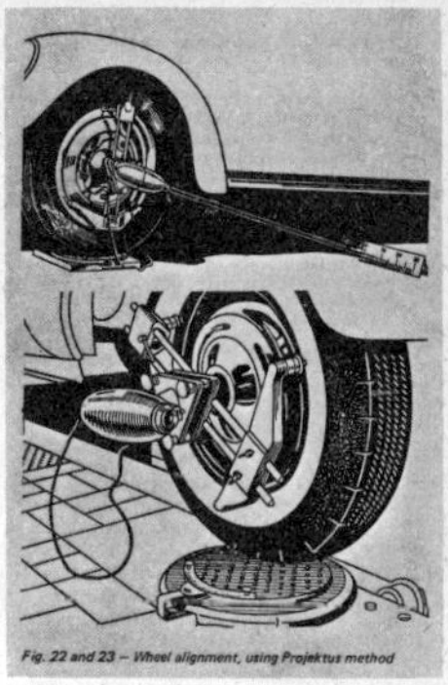

Fig. 22 and 23 – Wheel alignment, using Projektus method

A sample page from Automobile Fault Diagnosis

AUTOMOBILE ENGINE TESTING

ISBN: 0-903192-03-9 140 pages

This publication deals with the subject of engine testing from all aspects. It includes basic test operations, the use of sophisticated test equipment and the operation of diagnostic test bays. In all senses, this is a compact and informative work providing up-to-date knowledge on a vital topic. It also incorporates extensive fault-finding charts.
CONTENTS: Basic Testing — Battery Test — Spark Plug Test — Compression Test — Contact Breaker Test — Ignition Timing — Ignition Test — Condenser Test — Suppression Test — Engine Test — Cylinder Balancing — Feed Pump Test — Carburetter Adjustment — Exhaust Check — Generator Test — Test Equipment.

AUTOMOBILE FAULT DIAGNOSIS

ISBN: 0-903192-24-1 120 pages

Covers the basic fault diagnosis, repair and adjustment of motor vehicles based on current practices and equipment. Also includes fault-finding charts.
CONTENTS: Faults on the Engine — Cooling System — Lubrication System — Fuel System — Cylinders — Pistons — Rings and Connecting Rods — Crankshaft and Flywheel — Valve-Gear — Inlet and Exhaust Systems — Chassis — Clutch — Gearbox — Final Drive — Steering and Front Axle — Fibre Glass Bodies.

AUTOMOBILE PERFORMANCE TESTING

ISBN: 0-903192-07-1 150 pages

This is a companion volume to 'Automobile Engine Testing', giving equally extensive coverage to the subject of stationary and dynamic test methods for motor vehicles. The construction, function and operation of dynomometers and other vehicle test equipment is examined in detail.
CONTENTS: Function — Performance — Static Tests — Road Test — Dynomometer Tests — Fault-Finding.

AUTOMOBILE RADIO INTERFERENCE SUPPRESSION

ISBN: 0-903192-02-0 110 pages

An authoritative work describing the propogation of electrical interference and the various methods of suppression.
CONTENTS: Radios in Motor Vehicles — Radio Reception — Car Aerials — Radio Interference — Types of Suppression — Testing Close Range Interference Suppression — Extensive Fault-Finding Chart.

BOSCH ELECTRICAL SYSTEMS

ISBN 0-903192-06-3 184 pages

Not a purely theoretical write-up on Bosch Electrical Systems but a practical pocket guide for those concerned with working on them. The reader will find that in a very brief but extremely comprehensive way all the testing, trouble-shooting, servicing and repair instructions are given that are really required. A major feature of this book is the way in which it will help to diagnose faults rapidly and systematically.
Includes details of: Circuit Diagrams, Wiring Looms, Lighting Systems, Signalling Devices, Batteries, Generators, Coils, Spark Plugs, Starter Motors.

HOW TO ORDER
Motobooks

Whenever you wish to purchase any of the listed books take this form to your Bookseller or Motorshop who will order the book for you. If this is not possible, mail the order form to us with your payment and we will send the required books to you by return.

Please observe the following instructions:

ORDERING BOOKS BY MAIL from

ALBION SCOTT LTD.
Bercourt House
51 York Road
Brentford Middx
TW8 OQP England

Identify required books on this form.
Mail complete form to us, with your remittance (either cheque, postal order or cash) to which you must add the postage as set out below.

Make sure that your
NAME and ADDRESS is given in the space below.

Postage and Packing:

		UK	EUROPE	OVERSEAS
Book price to	£2.00	10p	15p	20p
	£3.00	15p	20p	25p
over	£3.00	20p	30p	40p

Dispatch by surface book mail only.

Name ....

Address ....

Special Instructions ....

Get your facts straight from a Motobook

SPECIAL TITLES FROM ALBION SCOTT

Qty.	Title	Price	Total
	SPEEDSPORT		
	Tuning SU Carburetters	£1.00	
	Tuning Weber, Vol. 1	70p	
	Tuning Weber, Vol. 2	£1.00	
	Tuning Stromberg Carbs.	50p	
	Tuning Solex Carburetters	£1.30	
	Tuning Zenith Carburetters	£1.00	
	Tuning the Mini	£1.20	
	More Mini Tuning	£1.30	
	Tuning Four Cyl. Fords	£1.50	
	Tuning Anglias and Cortinas	£1.00	
	Tuning Twin Cam Fords	£1.00	
	Tuning Escorts and Capris	£1.00	
	Tuning Vivas & Firenzas	£1.30	
	Tuning BMC Sports Cars	£1.00	
	Triumphs to 1300 cc	70p	
	Tuning Triumphs over 1300 cc	£1.60	
	Tuning the VW	£1.50	
	Tuning V8 Engines	£1.80	
	How to Start Rallying	£1.00	
	Barry Lee Hot Rod	£1.00	
	How to Start Motor Racing	£1.00	
	How to Start Autocross	£1.00	
	Prod. Motorcy. Racing	£1.00	
	Introduction to Tuning	70p	
	Engines and Transm.	70p	
	Suspensions and Brakes	70p	
	Auto Electrics	£1.50	
	Lucas Ignition Systems	£1.00	
	Modif. Prod. Cy. Heads	70p	
	Racing Engine Prep.	£1.20	
	Car Customising	£1.00	
	High Speed Driving	£1.50	
	Cylinder Head Modific.	£1.50	
	Chassis Tuning	£1.50	
	Motorcycle Engineering	£2.25	
	The Big Drive	50p	
	Castrol Book of Car Care	25p	
	Motorcycle Care	25p	
	Qty TOTAL Price		

Qty.	Title	Price	Total
	INTERAUTO		
	Fault Diagnosis	£1.15	
	Interference Suppression	£1.15	
	Body and Paintwork	£1.15	
	Performance Testing	£1.15	
	Engine Testing	£1.15	
	Bosch Electrical Systems	£1.15	
	Caravan Service Manual	£1.15	
	SU Carburetters	£1.15	
	Solex Carburetters (Vol. 1)	£1.15	
	Zenith Carburetters	£1.15	
	Stromberg Carburetters	£1.15	
	Alternator Manual	£3.00	
	Petrol Fuel Injection	£4.50	
	CRYPTON		
	Engine and Electrical	£3.00	
	Corrective Service	£2.50	
	Diagnostic Wallchart	£2.50	
	WORKSHOP MANUALS		
	quote make, model & year		
	Cars	£2.50	
	Motorcycles	£2.00	
	HANDBOOKS		
	quote make, model & year	75p	
	Motorist Emergency Signs	75p	
	Motobook Catalogue	20p	
	Qty TOTAL Price		

NOTES

Albion Scott Ltd., 51 York Road, Brentford, Middlesex, TW8 0QP
England